How to Listen to Music

by Henry Edward

TO

W.J. HENDERSON

WHO HAS HELPED ME TO RESPECT MUSICAL CRITICISM

AUTHOR'S NOTE

The author is beholden to the Messrs. Harper & Brothers for permission to use a small portion of the material in Chapter I., the greater part of Chapter IV., and the Plates which were printed originally in one of their publications; also to the publishers of "The Looker-On" for the privilege of reprinting a portion of an essay written for them entitled "Singers, Then and Now."

CONTENTS

[Sidenote: CHAP. I.]

Introduction

Purpose and scope of this book--Not written for professional musicians, but for untaught lovers of the art--neither for careless seekers after diversion unless they be willing to accept a higher conception of what "entertainment" means--The capacity properly to listen to music as a touchstone of musical talent--It is rarely found in popular concert-rooms--Travellers who do not see and listeners who do not hear--Music is of all the arts that which is practised most and thought about least--Popular ignorance of the art caused by the lack of an object for comparison--How simple terms are confounded by literary men--Blunders by Tennyson, Lamb, Coleridge, Mrs. Harriet Beecher Stowe, F. Hopkinson Smith, Brander Matthews, and others--A warning against pedants and rhapsodists.

[Sidenote: CHAP. II.]

Recognition of Musical Elements

The dual nature of music--Sense-perception, fancy, and imagination--Recognition of Design as Form in its primary stages--The crude materials of music--The co-ordination of tones--Rudimentary analysis of Form--Comparison, as in other arts, not possible--Recognition of the fundamental elements--Melody, Harmony, and Rhythm--The value of memory--The need of an intermediary--Familiar music best liked--Interrelation of the elements--Repetition the fundamental principle of Form--Motives, Phrases, and Periods--A Creole folk-tune analyzed--Repetition at the base of poetic forms--Refrain and Parallelism--Key-relationship as a bond of union--Symphonic unity illustrated in examples from Beethoven--The C minor symphony and "Appassionata" sonata--The Concerto in G major--The Seventh and Ninth symphonies.

[Sidenote: CHAP. III.]

The Content and Kinds of Music

How far it is necessary for the listener to go into musical philosophy--Intelligent hearing not conditioned upon it--Man's individual relationship to the art--Musicians proceed on the theory that feelings are the content of music--The search for pictures and stories condemned--How composers hear and judge--Definitions of the capacity of music by Wagner, Hauptmann, and Mendelssohn--An utterance by Herbert Spencer--Music as a language--Absolute music and Programme music--The content of all true art works--Chamber music--Meaning and origin of the term--Haydn the servant of a Prince--The characteristics of Chamber music--Pure thought, lofty imagination, and deep learning--Its chastity--Sympathy between performers and listeners essential to its enjoyment--A correct definition of Programme music--Programme music defended--The value of titles and superscriptions--Judgment upon it must, however, go to the music, not the commentary--Subjects that are unfit for music--Kinds of Programme music--Imitative music--How the music of birds has been utilized--The cuckoo of nature and Beethoven's cuckoo--Cock and hen in a seventeenth century composition--Rameau's pullet--The German quail--Music that is descriptive by suggestion--External and internal attributes--Fancy and Imagination--Harmony and the major and minor mode--Association of ideas--Movement delineated--Handel's frogs--Water in the "Hebrides" overture and "Ocean" symphony--Height and depth illustrated by acute and grave tones--Beethoven's illustration of distance--His rule enforced--Classical and Romantic music--Genesis of the terms--What they mean in literature--Archbishop Trench on classical books--The author's definitions of both terms in music--Classicism as the conservative principle, Romanticism as the progressive, regenerative, and creative--A contest which stimulates life.

[Sidenote: CHAP. IV.]

The Modern Orchestra

Importance of the instrumental band--Some things that can be learned by its study--The orchestral choirs--Disposition of the players--Model bands compared--Development of instrumental music--The extent of an orchestra's register--The Strings: Violin, Viola, Violoncello, and Double-bass--Effects produced by changes in manipulation--The wood-winds: Flute, Oboe, English horn, Bassoon, Clarinet--The Brass: French Horn, Trumpet and Cornet, Trombone, Tuba--The Drums--The Conductor--Rise of the modern interpreter--The need of him--His methods--Scores and Score-reading.

[Sidenote: CHAP. V.]

At an Orchestral Concert

"Classical" and "Popular" as generally conceived--Symphony Orchestras and Military bands--The higher forms in music as exemplified at a classical concert--Symphonies, Overtures, Symphonic Poems, Concertos, etc.--A Symphony not a union of unrelated parts--History of the name--The Sonata form and cyclical compositions--The bond of union between the divisions of a Symphony--Material and spiritual links--The first movement and the sonata form--"Exposition, illustration, and repetition"--The subjects and their treatment--Keys and nomenclature of the Symphony--The Adagio or second movement--The Scherzo and its relation to the Minuet--The Finale and the Rondo form--The latter illustrated in outline by a poem--Modifications of the symphonic form by Beethoven, Schumann, Berlioz, Mendelssohn, Liszt, Saint-Saëns and Dvorak--Augmentation of the forces--Symphonies with voices--The Symphonic Poem--Its three characteristics--Concertos and Cadenzas--M. Ysaye's opinion of the latter--Designations in Chamber music--The Overture and its descendants--Smaller forms: Serenades, Fantasias, Rhapsodies, Variations, Operatic Excerpts.

[Sidenote: CHAP. VI.]

At a Pianoforte Recital

The Popularity of Pianoforte music exemplified in M. Paderewski's recitals--The instrument--A universal medium of music study--Its defects and merits contrasted--Not a perfect melody instrument--Value of the percussive element--Technique; the false and the true estimate of its value--Pianoforte literature as illustrated in recitals--Its division, for the purposes of this study, into four periods: Classic, Classic-romantic, Romantic, and Bravura--Precursors of the Pianoforte--The Clavichord and Harpsichord, and the music composed for them--Peculiarities of Bach's style--His Romanticism--Scarlatti's Sonatas--The Suite and its constituents--Allemande, Courante, Sarabande, Gigue, Minuet, and Gavotte--The technique of the period--How Bach and Handel played--Beethoven and the Sonata--Mozart and Beethoven as pianists--The Romantic composers--Schumann and Chopin and the forms used by them--Schumann and Jean Paul--Chopin's Preludes, Etudes, Nocturnes, Ballades, Polonaises, Mazurkas, Krakowiak--The technique of the Romantic period--"Idiomatic" pianoforte music--Development of the instrument--The Pedal and its use--Liszt and his Hungarian Rhapsodies.

[Sidenote: CHAP. VII.]

At the Opera

Instability of popular taste in respect of operas--Our lists seldom extend back of the present century--The people of to-day as indifferent as those of two centuries ago to the language used--Use and abuse of foreign languages--The Opera defended as an art-form--Its origin in the Greek tragedies--Why music is the language of emotion--A scientific explanation--Herbert Spencer's laws--Efforts of Florentine scholars to revive the classic tragedy result in the invention of the lyric drama--The various kinds of Opera: Opera seria, Opera buffa, Opera semiseria, French grand Opera, and _Opera comique_--Operettas and musical farces--Romantic Opera--A popular conception of German opera--A return to the old terminology led by Wagner--The recitative: Its nature, aims, and capacities--The change from speech to song--The arioso style, the accompanied recitative and the aria--Music and dramatic action--Emancipation from set forms--The orchestra--The decay of singing--Feats of the masters of the Roman school and La Bastardella--Degeneracy of the Opera of their day--Singers who have been heard in New York--Two generations of singers compared--Grisi, Jenny Lind, Sontag, La Grange, Piccolomini, Adelina Patti, Nilsson, Sembrich, Lucca, Gerster, Lehmann, Melba, Eames, Calv? Mario, Jean and Edouard de Reszke--Wagner and his works--Operas and lyric dramas--Wagner's return to the principles of the Florentine reformers--Interdependence of elements in a lyric drama--Forms and the endless melody--The Typical Phrases: How they should be studied.

[Sidenote: CHAP. VIII.]

Choirs and Choral Music

Value of chorus singing in musical culture--Schumann's advice to students--Choristers and instrumentalists--Amateurs and professionals--Oratorio and Männergesang--The choirs of Handel and Bach--Glee Unions, Male Clubs, and Women's Choirs--Boys' voices not adapted to modern music--Mixed choirs--American Origin of amateur singing societies--Priority over Germany--The size of choirs--Large numbers not essential--How choirs are divided--Antiphonal effects--Excellence in choir singing--Precision, intonation, expression, balance of tone, enunciation, pronunciation, declamation--The cause of monotony in Oratorio performances--_A capella_ music--Genesis of modern hymnology--Influence of Luther and the Germans--Use of popular melodies by composers--The chorale--Preservation of the severe style of writing in choral music--Palestrina and Bach--A study of their styles--Latin and Teuton--Church and individual--Motets and Church Cantatas--The Passions--The Oratorio--Sacred opera and Cantata--Epic and Drama--Characteristic and descriptive music--The Mass: Its secularization and musical development--The dramatic tendency illustrated in Beethoven and Berlioz.

[Sidenote: CHAP. IX.]

Musician, Critic and Public

Criticism justified--Relationship between Musician, Critic and Public--To end the conflict between them would result in stagnation--How the Critic might escape--The Musician prefers to appeal to the public rather than to the Critic--Why this is so--Ignorance as a safeguard against and promoter of conservatism--Wagner and Haydn--The Critic as the enemy of the charlatan--Temptations to which he is exposed--Value of popular approbation--Schumann's aphorisms--The Public neither bad judges nor good critics--The Critic's duty is to guide popular judgment--Fickleness of the people's opinions--Taste and judgment not a birthright--The necessity of antecedent study--The Critic's responsibility--Not always that toward the Musician which the latter thinks--How the newspaper can work for good--Must the Critic be a Musician?--Pedants and Rhapsodists--Demonstrable facts in criticism--The folly and viciousness of foolish rhapsody--The Rev. Mr. Haweis cited--Ernst's violin--Intelligent rhapsody approved--Dr. John Brown on Beethoven--The Critic's duty.

How to Listen to Music

I

Introduction

[Sidenote: The book's appeal.]

This book has a purpose, which is as simple as it is plain; and an unpretentious scope. It does not aim to edify either the musical professor or the musical scholar. It comes into the presence of the musical student with all becoming modesty. Its business is with those who love music and present themselves for its gracious ministrations in Concert-Room and Opera House, but have not studied it as professors and scholars are supposed to study. It is not for the careless unless they be willing to inquire whether it might not be well to yield the common conception of entertainment in favor of the higher enjoyment which springs from serious contemplation of beautiful things; but if they are willing so to inquire, they shall be accounted the class that the author is most anxious to reach. The reasons which prompted its writing and the laying out of its plan will presently appear. For the frankness of his disclosure the author might be willing to apologize were his reverence for music less and his consideration for popular affectations more; but because he is convinced that a love for music carries with it that which, so it be but awakened, shall speedily grow into an honest desire to know more about the beloved object, he is willing to seem unamiable to the amateur while arguing the need of even so mild a stimulant as his book, and ingenuous, mayhap even childish, to the professional musician while trying to point a way in which better appreciation may be sought.

[Sidenote: Talent in listening.]

The capacity properly to listen to music is better proof of musical talent in the listener than skill to play upon an instrument or ability to sing acceptably when unaccompanied by that capacity. It makes more for that gentleness and refinement of emotion, thought, and action which, in the highest sense of the term, it is the province of music to promote. And it is a much rarer accomplishment. I cannot conceive anything more pitiful than the spectacle of men and women perched on a fair observation point exclaiming rapturously at the loveliness of mead and valley, their eyes melting involuntarily in tenderness at the sight of moss-carpeted slopes and rocks and peaceful wood, or dilating in reverent wonder at mountain magnificence, and then learning from their exclamations that, as a matter of fact, they are unable to distinguish between rock and tree, field and forest, earth and sky; between the dark-browns of the storm-scarred rock, the greens of the foliage, and the blues of the sky.

[Sidenote: Ill equipped listeners.]

Yet in the realm of another sense, in the contemplation of beauties more ethereal and evanescent than those of nature, such is the experience which in my capacity as a writer for newspapers I have made for many years. A party of people blind to form and color cannot be said to be well equipped for a Swiss journey, though loaded down with alpenstocks and Baedekers; yet the spectacle of such a party on the top of the Rigi is no more pitiful and anomalous than that presented by the majority of the hearers in our concert-rooms. They are there to adventure a journey into a realm whose beauties do not disclose themselves to the senses alone, but whose perception requires a co-operation of all the finer faculties; yet of this they seem to know nothing, and even of that sense to which the first appeal is made it may be said with profound truth that "hearing they hear not, neither do they understand."

[Sidenote: Popular ignorance of music.]

Of all the arts, music is practised most and thought about least. Why this should be the case may be explained on several grounds. A sweet mystery enshrouds the nature of music. Its material part is subtle and elusive. To master it on its technical side alone costs a vast expenditure of time, patience, and industry. But since it is, in one manifestation or another, the most popular of the arts, and one the enjoyment of which is conditioned in a peculiar degree on love, it remains passing strange that the indifference touching its nature and elements, and the character of the phenomena which produce it, or are produced by it, is so general. I do not recall that anybody has ever tried to ground this popular ignorance touching an art of which, by right of birth, everybody is a critic. The unamiable nature of the task, of which I am keenly conscious, has probably been a bar to such an undertaking. But a frank diagnosis must precede the discovery of a cure for every disease, and I have undertaken to point out a way in which this grievous ailment in the social body may at least be lessened.

[Sidenote: Paucity of intelligent comment.]

[Sidenote: Want of a model.]

It is not an exaggeration to say that one might listen for a lifetime to the polite conversation of our drawing-rooms (and I do not mean by this to refer to the United States alone) without hearing a symphony talked about in terms indicative of more than the most superficial knowledge of the outward form, that is, the dimensions and apparatus, of such a composition. No other art provides an exact analogy for this phenomenon. Everybody can say something containing a degree of appositeness about a poem, novel, painting, statue, or building. If he can do no more he can go as far as Landseer's rural critic who objected to one of the artist's paintings on the ground that not one of the three pigs eating from a trough had a foot in it. It is the absence of the standard of judgment employed in this criticism which makes significant talk about music so difficult. Nature failed to provide a model for this ethereal art. There is nothing in the natural world with which the simple man may compare it.

[Sidenote: Simple terms confounded.]

It is not alone a knowledge of the constituent factors of a symphony, or the difference between a sonata and a suite, a march and a mazurka, that is rare. Unless you chance to be listening to the conversation of musicians (in which term I wish to include amateurs who are what the word amateur implies, and whose knowledge stands in some respectable relation to their love), you will find, so frequently that I have not the heart to attempt an estimate of the proportion, that the most common words in the terminology of the art are misapplied. Such familiar things as harmony and melody, time and tune, are continually confounded. Let us call a distinguished witness into the box; the instance is not new, but it will serve. What does Tennyson mean when he says:

"All night have the roses heard The flute, violin, bassoon; All night has the casement jessamine stirr'd To the dancers dancing in tune?"

[Sidenote: Tune and time.]

Unless the dancers who wearied Maud were provided with even a more extraordinary instrumental outfit than the Old Lady of Banbury Cross, how could they have danced "in tune?"

[Sidenote: Blunders of poets and essayists.]

Musical study of a sort being almost as general as study of the "three Rs," it must be said that the gross forms of ignorance are utterly inexcusable. But if this is obvious, it is even more obvious that there is something radically wrong with the prevalent systems of musical instruction. It is because of a plentiful lack of knowledge that so much that is written on music is without meaning, and that the most foolish kind of rhapsody, so it show a collocation of fine words, is permitted to masquerade as musical criticism and even analysis. People like to read about music, and the books of a certain English clergyman have had a sale of stupendous magnitude notwithstanding they are full of absurdities. The clergyman has a multitudinous companionship, moreover, among novelists, essayists, and poets whose safety lies in more or less fantastic generalization when they come to talk about music. How they flounder when they come to detail! It was Charles Lamb who said, in his "Chapter on Ears," that in voices he could not distinguish a soprano from a tenor, and could only contrive to guess at the thorough-bass from its being "supereminently harsh and disagreeable;" yet dear old Elia may be forgiven, since his confounding the bass voice with a system of musical short-hand is so delightful a proof of the ignorance he was confessing.

[Sidenote: Literary realism and musical terminology.]

But what shall the troubled critics say to Tennyson's orchestra consisting of a flute, violin, and bassoon? Or to Coleridge's "loud bassoon," which made the wedding-guest to beat his breast? Or to Mrs. Harriet Beecher Stowe's pianist who played "with an airy and bird-like touch?" Or to our own clever painter-novelist who, in "Snubbin' through Jersey," has Brushes bring out his violoncello and play "the symphonies of Beethoven" to entertain his fellow canal-boat passengers? The tendency toward realism, or "veritism," as it is called, has brought out a rich crop of blunders. It will not do to have a character in a story simply sing or play something; we must have the names of composers and compositions. The genial gentleman who enriched musical literature with arrangements of Beethoven's symphonies for violoncello without accompaniment has since supplemented this feat by creating a German fiddler who, when he thinks himself unnoticed, plays a sonata for violin and contralto voice; Professor Brander Matthews permits one of his heroines to sing Schumann's "Warum?" and one of his heroes plays "The Moonlight Concerto;" one of Ouida's romantic creatures spends hours at an organ "playing the grand old masses of Mendelssohn;" in "Moths" the tenor never wearies of singing certain "exquisite airs of Palestrina," which recalls the fact that an indignant correspondent of a St. Louis newspaper, protesting against the Teutonism and heaviness of an orchestra conductor's programmes, demanded some of the "lighter" works of "Berlioz and Palestrina."

[Sidenote: A popular need.]

Alas! these things and the many others equally amusing which Mr. G. Sutherland Edwards long ago catalogued in an essay on "The Literary Maltreatment of Music" are but evidences that even cultured folk have not yet learned to talk correctly about the art which is practised most widely. There is a greater need than pianoforte teachers and singing teachers, and that is a numerous company of writers and talkers who shall teach the people how to listen to music so that it shall not pass through their heads like a vast tonal phantasmagoria, but provide the varied and noble delights contemplated by the composers.

[Sidenote: A warning against writers.]

[Sidenote: Pedants and rhapsodists.]

Ungracious as it might appear, it may yet not be amiss, therefore, at the very outset of an inquiry into the proper way in which to listen to music, to utter a warning against much that is written on the art. As a rule it will be found that writers on music are divided into two classes, and that neither of these classes can do much good. Too often they are either pedants or rhapsodists. This division is wholly natural. Music has many sides and is a science as well as an art. Its scientific side is that on which the pedant generally approaches it. He is concerned with forms and rules, with externals, to the forgetting of that which is inexpressibly nobler and higher. But the pedants are not harmful, because they are not interesting; strictly speaking, they do not write for the public at all, but only for their professional colleagues. The harmful men are the foolish rhapsodists who take advantage of the fact that the language of music is indeterminate and evanescent to talk about the art in such a way as to present themselves as persons of exquisite sensibilities rather than to direct attention to the real nature and beauty of music itself. To them I shall recur in a later chapter devoted to musical criticism, and haply point out the difference between good and bad critics and commentators from the view-point of popular need and popular opportunity.

II

Recognition of Musical Elements

[Sidenote: The nature of music.]

Music is dual in its nature; it is material as well as spiritual. Its material side we apprehend through the sense of hearing, and comprehend through the intellect; its spiritual side reaches us through the fancy (or imagination, so it be music of the highest class), and the emotional part of us. If the scope and capacity of the art, and the evolutionary processes which its history discloses (a record of which is preserved in its nomenclature), are to be understood, it is essential that this duality be kept in view. There is something so potent and elemental in the appeal which music makes that it is possible to derive pleasure from even an unwilling hearing or a hearing unaccompanied by effort at analysis; but real appreciation of its beauty, which means recognition of the qualities which put it in the realm of art, is conditioned upon intelligent hearing. The higher the intelligence, the keener will be the enjoyment, if the former be directed to the spiritual side as well as the material.

[Sidenote: Necessity of intelligent hearing.]

So far as music is merely agreeably co-ordinated sounds, it may be reduced to mathematics and its practice to handicraft. But recognition of design is a condition precedent to the awakening of the fancy or the imagination, and to achieve such recognition there must be intelligent hearing in the first instance. For the purposes of this study, design may be held to be Form in its primary stages, the recognition of which is possible to every listener who is fond of music; it is not necessary that he be learned in the science. He need only be willing to let an intellectual process, which will bring its own reward, accompany the physical process of hearing.

[Sidenote: Tones and musical material.]

Without discrimination it is impossible to recognize even the crude materials of music, for the first step is already a co-ordination of those materials. A tone becomes musical material only by association with another tone. We might hear it alone, study its quality, and determine its degree of acuteness or gravity (its pitch, as musicians say), but it can never become music so long as it remains isolated. When we recognize that it bears certain relationships with other tones in respect of time or tune (to use simple terms), it has become for us musical material. We do not need to philosophize about the nature of those relationships, but we must recognize their existence.

[Sidenote: The beginnings of Form.]

Thus much we might hear if we were to let music go through our heads like water through a sieve. Yet the step from that degree of discrimination to a rudimentary analysis of Form is exceedingly short, and requires little more than a willingness to concentrate the attention and exercise the memory. Everyone is willing to do that much while looking at a picture. Who would look at a painting and rest satisfied with the impression made upon the sense of sight by the colors merely? No one, surely. Yet so soon as we look, so as to discriminate between the outlines, to observe the relationship of figure to figure, we are indulging in intellectual exercise. If this be a condition precedent to the enjoyment of a picture (and it plainly is), how much more so is it in the case of music, which is intangible and evanescent, which cannot pause a moment for our contemplation without ceasing to be?

[Sidenote: Comparison with a model not possible.]

There is another reason why we must exercise intelligence in listening, to which I have already alluded in the first chapter. Our appreciation of beauty in the plastic arts is helped by the circumstance that the critical activity is largely a matter of comparison. Is the picture or the statue a good copy of the object sought to be represented? Such comparison fails us utterly in music, which copies nothing that is tangibly present in the external world.

[Sidenote: What degree of knowledge is necessary?]

[Sidenote: The Elements.]

[Sidenote: Value of memory.]

It is then necessary to associate the intellect with sense perception in listening to music. How far is it essential that the intellectual process shall go? This book being for the untrained, the question might be put thus: With how little knowledge of the science can an intelligent listener get along? We are concerned only with his enjoyment of music or, better, with an effort to increase it without asking him to become a musician. If he is fond of the art it is more than likely that the capacity to discriminate sufficiently to recognize the elements out of which music is made has come to him intuitively. Does he recognize that musical tones are related to each other in respect of time and pitch? Then it shall not be difficult for him to recognize the three elements on which music rests--Melody, Harmony, and Rhythm. Can he recognize them with sufficient distinctness to seize upon their manifestations while music is sounding? Then memory shall come to the aid of discrimination, and he shall be able to appreciate enough of design to point the way to a true and lofty appreciation of the beautiful in music. The value of memory is for obvious reasons very great in musical enjoyment. The picture remains upon the wall, the book upon the library shelf. If we have failed to grasp a detail at the first glance or reading, we need but turn again to the picture or open the book anew. We may see the picture in a changed light, or read the poem in a different mood, but the outlines, colors, ideas are fixed for frequent and patient perusal. Music goes out of existence with every performance, and must be recreated at every hearing.

[Sidenote: An intermediary necessary.]

Not only that, but in the case of all, so far as some forms are concerned, and of all who are not practitioners in others, it is necessary that there shall be an intermediary between the composer and the listener. The written or printed notes are not music; they are only signs which indicate to the performer what to do to call tones into existence such as the composer had combined into an art-work in his mind. The broadly trained musician can read the symbols; they stir his imagination, and he hears the music in his imagination as the composer heard it. But the untaught music-lover alone can get nothing from the printed page; he must needs wait till some one else shall again waken for him the

"Sound of a voice that is still."

[Sidenote: The value of memory.]

This is one of the drawbacks which are bound up in the nature of music; but it has ample compensation in the unusual pleasure which memory brings. In the case of the best music, familiarity breeds ever-growing admiration. New compositions are slowly received; they make their way to popular appreciation only by repeated performances; the people like best the songs as well as the symphonies which they know. The quicker, therefore, that we are in recognizing the melodic, harmonic, and rhythmic contents of a new composition, and the more apt our memory in seizing upon them for the operation of the fancy, the greater shall be our pleasure.

[Sidenote: Melody, Harmony, and Rhythm.]

[Sidenote: Comprehensiveness of Melody.]

In simple phrase Melody is a well-ordered series of tones heard successively; Harmony, a well-ordered series heard simultaneously; Rhythm, a symmetrical grouping of tonal time units vitalized by accent. The life-blood of music is Melody, and a complete conception of the term embodies within itself the essence of both its companions. A succession of tones without harmonic regulation is not a perfect element in music; neither is a succession of tones which have harmonic regulation but are void of rhythm. The beauty and expressiveness, especially the emotionality, of a musical composition depend upon the harmonies which either accompany the melody in the form of chords (a group of melodic intervals sounded simultaneously), or are latent in the melody itself (harmonic intervals sounded successively). Melody is Harmony analyzed; Harmony is Melody synthetized.

[Sidenote: Repetition.]

[Sidenote: A melody analyzed.]

The fundamental principle of Form is repetition of melodies, which are to music what ideas are to poetry. Melodies themselves are made by repetition of smaller fractions called motives (a term borrowed from the fine arts), phrases, and periods, which derive their individuality from their rhythmical or intervallic characteristics. Melodies are not all of the simple kind which the musically illiterate, or the musically ill-trained, recognize as "tunes," but they all have a symmetrical organization. The dissection of a simple folk-tune may serve to make this plain and also indicate to the untrained how a single feature may be taken as a mark of identification and a holding-point for the memory. Here is the melody of a Creole song called sometimes Pov' piti Lolotte, sometimes _Pov' piti Momzelle Zizi_, in the patois of Louisiana and Martinique:

[Sidenote: Motives, phrases, and periods.]

It will be as apparent to the eye of one who cannot read music as it will to his ear when he hears this melody played, that it is built up of two groups of notes only. These groups are marked off by the heavy lines across the staff called bars, whose purpose it is to indicate rhythmical subdivisions in music. The second, third, fifth, sixth, and seventh of these groups are repetitions merely of the first group, which is the germ of the melody, but on different degrees of the scale; the fourth and eighth groups are identical and are an appendage hitched to the first group for the purpose of bringing it to a close, supplying a resting-point craved by man's innate sense of symmetry. Musicians call such groups cadences. A musical analyst would call each group a motive, and say that each successive two groups, beginning with the first, constitute a phrase, each two phrases a period, and the two periods a melody. We have therefore in this innocent Creole tune eight motives, four phrases, and two periods; yet its material is summed up in two groups, one of seven notes, one of five, which only need to be identified and remembered to enable a listener to recognize something of the design of a composer if he were to put the melody to the highest purposes that melody can be put in the art of musical composition.

[Sidenote: Repetition in music.]

Repetition is the constructive principle which was employed by the folk-musician in creating this melody; and repetition is the fundamental principle in all musical construction. It will suffice for many merely to be reminded of this to appreciate the fact that while the exercise of memory is a most necessary activity in listening to music, it lies in music to make that exercise easy. There is repetition of motives, phrases, and periods in melody; repetition of melodies in parts; and repetition of parts in the wholes of the larger forms.

[Sidenote: Repetition in poetry.]

The beginnings of poetic forms are also found in repetition; in primitive poetry it is exemplified in the refrain or burden, in the highly developed poetry of the Hebrews in parallelism. The Psalmist wrote:

"O Lord, rebuke me not in thy wrath, Neither chasten me in thy hot displeasure."

[Sidenote: Key relationship.]

Here is a period of two members, the latter repeating the thought of the former. A musical analyst might find in it an admirable analogue for the first period of a simple melody. He would divide it into four motives: "Rebuke me not | in thy wrath | neither chasten me | in thy hot displeasure," and point out as intimate a relationship between them as exists in the Creole tune. The bond of union between the motives of the melody as well as that in the poetry illustrates a principle of beauty which is the most important element in musical design after repetition, which is its necessary vehicle. It is because this principle guides the repetition of the tone-groups that together they form a melody that is perfect, satisfying, and reposeful. It is the principle of key-relationship, to discuss which fully would carry me farther into musical science than I am permitted to go. Let this suffice: A harmony is latent in each group, and the sequence of groups is such a sequence as the experience of ages has demonstrated to be most agreeable to the ear.

[Sidenote: The rhythmical stamp.]

[Sidenote: The principle of Unity.]

In the case of the Creole melody the listener is helped to a quick appreciation of its form by the distinct physiognomy which rhythm has stamped upon it; and it is by noting such a characteristic that the memory can best be aided in its work of identification. It is not necessary for a listener to follow all the processes of a composer in order to enjoy his music, but if he cultivates the habit of following the principal themes through a work of the higher class he will not only enjoy the pleasures of memory but will frequently get a glimpse into the composer's purposes which will stimulate his imagination and mightily increase his enjoyment. There is nothing can guide him more surely to a recognition of the principle of unity, which makes a symphony to be an organic whole instead of a group of pieces which are only externally related. The greatest exemplar of this principle is Beethoven; and his music is the best in which to study it for the reason that he so frequently employs material signs for the spiritual bond. So forcibly has this been impressed upon me at times that I am almost willing to believe that a keen analytical student of his music might arrange his greater works into groups of such as were in process of composition at the same time without reference to his personal history. Take the principal theme of the C minor Symphony for example:

[Sidenote: A rhythmical motive pursued.]

This simple, but marvellously pregnant, motive is not only the kernel of the first movement, it is the fundamental thought of the whole symphony. We hear its persistent beat in the scherzo as well:

and also in the last movement:

More than this, we find the motive haunting the first movement of the pianoforte sonata in F minor, op. 57, known as the "Sonata Appassionata," now gloomily, almost morosely, proclamative in the bass, now interrogative in the treble:

[Sidenote: Relationships in Beethoven's works.]

[Sidenote: The C minor Symphony and "Appassionata" sonata.]

[Sidenote: Beethoven's G major Concerto.]

Schindler relates that when once he asked Beethoven to tell him what the F minor and the D minor (Op. 31, No. 2) sonatas meant, he received for an answer only the enigmatical remark: "Read Shakespeare's 'Tempest.'" Many a student and commentator has since read the "Tempest" in the hope of finding a clew to the emotional contents which Beethoven believed to be in the two works, so singularly associated, only to find himself baffled. It is a fancy, which rests perhaps too much on outward things, but still one full of suggestion, that had Beethoven said: "Hear my C minor Symphony," he would have given a better starting-point to the imagination of those who are seeking to know what the F minor sonata means. Most obviously it means music, but it means music that is an expression of one of those psychological struggles which Beethoven felt called upon more and more to delineate as he was more and more shut out from the companionship of the external world. Such struggles are in the truest sense of the word tempests. The motive, which, according to the story, Beethoven himself said indicates, in the symphony, the rappings of Fate at the door of human existence, is common to two works which are also related in their spiritual contents. Singularly enough, too, in both cases the struggle which is begun in the first movement and continued in the third, is interrupted by a period of calm reassuring, soul-fortifying aspiration, which in the symphony as well as in the sonata takes the form of a theme with variations. Here, then, the recognition of a simple rhythmical figure has helped us to an appreciation of the spiritual unity of the parts of a symphony, and provided a commentary on the poetical contents of a sonata. But the lesson is not yet exhausted. Again do we find the rhythm coloring the first movement of the pianoforte concerto in G major:

Symphony, concerto, and sonata, as the sketch-books of the master show, were in process of creation at the same time.

[Sidenote: His Seventh Symphony.]

Thus far we have been helped in identifying a melody and studying relationships by the rhythmical structure of a single motive. The demonstration might be extended on the same line into Beethoven's symphony in A major, in which the external sign of the poetical idea which underlies the whole work is also rhythmic--so markedly so that Wagner characterized it most happily and truthfully when he said that it was "the apotheosis of the dance." Here it is the dactyl, [dactyl symbol], which in one variation, or another, clings to us almost as persistently as in Hood's "Bridge of Sighs:"

"One more unfortunate Weary of breath, Rashly importunate, Gone to her death."

[Sidenote: Use of a dactylic figure.]

We hear it lightly tripping in the first movement:

[Music illustration] and [Music illustration];

gentle, sedate, tender, measured, through its combination with a spondee in the second:

cheerily, merrily, jocosely happy in the Scherzo:

hymn-like in the Trio:

and wildly bacchanalian when subjected to trochaic abbreviation in the Finale:

[Sidenote: Intervallic characteristics.]

Intervallic characteristics may place the badge of relationship upon melodies as distinctly as rhythmic. There is no more perfect illustration of this than that afforded by Beethoven's Ninth Symphony. Speaking of the subject of its finale, Sir George Grove says:

"And note--while listening to the simple tune itself, before the variations begin--how very simple it is; the plain diatonic scale, not a single chromatic interval, and out of fifty-six notes only three not consecutive."[A]

[Sidenote: The melodies in Beethoven's Ninth Symphony.]

Earlier in the same work, while combating a statement by Lenz that the resemblance between the second subject of the first movement and the choral melody is a "thematic reference of the most striking importance, vindicating the unity of the entire work, and placing the whole in a perfectly new light," Sir George says:

"It is, however, very remarkable that so many of the melodies in the Symphony should consist of consecutive notes, and that in no less than four of them the notes should run up a portion of the scale and down again--apparently pointing to a consistent condition of Beethoven's mind throughout this work."

[Sidenote: Melodic likenesses.]

Like Goethe, Beethoven secreted many a mystery in his masterpiece, but he did not juggle idly with tones, or select the themes of his symphonies at haphazard; he would be open to the charge, however, if the resemblances which I have pointed out in the Fifth and Seventh Symphonies, and those disclosed by the following melodies from his Ninth, should turn out through some incomprehensible revelation to be mere coincidences:

From the first movement:

From the second:

The choral melody:

[Sidenote: Design and Form.]

From a recognition of the beginnings of design, to which identification of the composer's thematic material and its simpler relationships will lead, to so much knowledge of Form as will enable the reader to understand the later chapters in this book, is but a step.

FOOTNOTES:

[A] "Beethoven and His Nine Symphonies," p. 374.

III

The Content and Kinds of Music

[Sidenote: Metaphysics to be avoided herein.]

Bearing in mind the purpose of this book, I shall not ask the reader to accompany me far afield in the region of aesthetic philosophy or musical metaphysics. A short excursion is all that is necessary to make plain what is meant by such terms as Absolute music, Programme music, Classical, Romantic, and Chamber music and the like, which not only confront us continually in discussion, but stand for things which we must know if we would read programmes understandingly and appreciate the various phases in which music presents itself to us. It is interesting and valuable to know why an art-work stirs up pleasurable feelings within us, and to speculate upon its relations to the intellect and the emotions; but the circumstance that philosophers have never agreed, and probably never will agree, on these points, so far as the art of music is concerned, alone suffices to remove them from the field of this discussion.

[Sidenote: Personal equation in judgment.]

Intelligent listening is not conditioned upon such knowledge. Even when the study is begun, the questions whether or not music has a content beyond itself, where that content is to be sought, and how defined, will be decided in each case by the student for himself, on grounds which may be said to be as much in his nature as they are in the argument. The attitude of man toward the art is an individual one, and in some of its aspects defies explanation.

[Sidenote: A musical fluid.]

The amount and kind of pleasure which music gives him are frequently as much beyond his understanding and control as they are beyond the understanding and control of the man who sits beside him. They are consequences of just that particular combination of material and spiritual elements, just that blending of muscular, nervous, and cerebral tissues, which make him what he is, which segregate him as an individual from the mass of humanity. We speak of persons as susceptible or insusceptible to music as we speak of good and poor conductors of electricity; and the analogy implied here is particularly apt and striking. If we were still using the scientific terms of a few decades ago I should say that a musical fluid might yet be discovered and its laws correlated with those of heat, light, and electricity. Like them, when reduced to its lowest terms, music is a form of motion, and it should not be difficult on this analogy to construct a theory which would account for the physical phenomena which accompany the hearing of music in some persons, such as the recession of blood from the face, or an equally sudden suffusion of the same veins, a contraction of the scalp accompanied by chilliness or a prickling sensation, or that roughness of the skin called goose-flesh, "flesh moved by an idea, flesh horripilated by a thought."

[Sidenote: Origin of musical elements.]

[Sidenote: Feelings and counterpoint.]

It has been denied that feelings are the content of music, or that it is the mission of music to give expression to feelings; but the scientific fact remains that the fundamental elements of vocal music--pitch, quality, and dynamic intensity--are the results of feelings working upon the vocal organs; and even if Mr. Herbert Spencer's theory be rejected, it is too late now to deny that music is conceived by its creators as a language of the emotions and so applied by them. The German philosopher Herbarth sought to reduce the question to an absurdity by expressing surprise that musicians should still believe that feelings could be "the proximate cause of the rules of simple and double counterpoint;" but Dr. Stainer found a sufficient answer by accepting the proposition as put, and directing attention to the fact that the feelings of men having first decided what was pleasurable in polyphony, and the rules of counterpoint having afterward been drawn from specimens of pleasurable polyphony, it was entirely correct to say that feelings are the proximate cause of the laws of counterpoint.

[Sidenote: How composers hear music.]

It is because so many of us have been taught by poets and romancers to think that there is a picture of some kind, or a story in every piece of music, and find ourselves unable to agree upon the picture or the story in any given case, that confusion is so prevalent among the musical laity. Composers seldom find difficulty in understanding each other. They listen for beauty, and if they find it they look for the causes which have produced it, and in apprehending beauty and recognizing means and cause they unvolitionally rise to the plane whence a view of the composer's purposes is clear. Having grasped the mood of a composition and found that it is being sustained or varied in a manner accordant with their conceptions of beauty, they occupy themselves with another kind of differentiation altogether than the misled disciples of the musical rhapsodists who overlook the general design and miss the grand proclamation in their search for petty suggestions for pictures and stories among the details of the composition. Let musicians testify for us. In his romance, "Ein Gliklicher Abend," Wagner says:

[Sidenote: Wagner's axiom.]

"That which music expresses is eternal and ideal. It does not give voice to the passion, the love, the longing of this or the other individual, under these or the other circumstances, but to passion, love, longing itself."

Moritz Hauptmann says:

[Sidenote: Hauptmann's.]

"The same music will admit of the most varied verbal expositions, and of not one of them can it be correctly said that it is exhaustive, the right one, and contains the whole significance of the music. This significance is contained most definitely in the music itself. It is not music that is ambiguous; it says the same thing to everybody; it speaks to mankind and gives voice only to human feelings. Ambiguity only then makes its appearance when each person attempts to formulate in his manner the emotional impression which he has received, when he attempts to fix and hold the ethereal essence of music, to utter the unutterable."

[Sidenote: Mendelssohn's.]

[Sidenote: The "Songs without Words."]

Mendelssohn inculcated the same lesson in a letter which he wrote to a young poet who had given titles to a number of the composer's "Songs Without Words," and incorporated what he conceived to be their sentiments in a set of poems. He sent his work to Mendelssohn with the request that the composer inform the writer whether or not he had succeeded in catching the meaning of the music. He desired the information because "music's capacity for expression is so vague and indeterminate." Mendelssohn replied:

"You give the various numbers of the book such titles as 'I Think of Thee,' 'Melancholy,' 'The Praise of God,' 'A Merry Hunt.' I can scarcely say whether I thought of these or other things while composing the music. Another might find 'I Think of Thee' where you find 'Melancholy,' and a real huntsman might consider 'A Merry Hunt' a veritable 'Praise of God.' But this is not because, as you think, music is vague. On the contrary, I believe that musical expression is altogether too definite, that it reaches regions and dwells in them whither words cannot follow it and must necessarily go lame when they make the attempt as you would have them do."

[Sidenote: The tonal language.]

[Sidenote: Herbert Spencer's definition.]

[Sidenote: Natural expression.]

[Sidenote: Absolute music.]

If I were to try to say why musicians, great musicians, speak thus of their art, my explanation would be that they have developed, farther than the rest of mankind have been able to develop it, a language of tones, which, had it been so willed, might have been developed so as to fill the place now occupied by articulate speech. Herbert Spencer, though speaking purely as a scientific investigator, not at all as an artist, defined music as "a language of feelings which may ultimately enable men vividly and completely to impress on each other the emotions they experience from moment to moment." We rely upon speech to do this now, but ever and anon when, in a moment of emotional exaltation, we are deserted by the articulate word we revert to the emotional cry which antedates speech, and find that that cry is universally understood because it is universally felt. More than speech, if its primitive element of emotionality be omitted, more than the primitive language of gesture, music is a natural mode of expression. All three forms have attained their present stage of development through conventions. Articulate speech has led in the development; gesture once occupied a high plane (in the pantomimic dance of the ancients) but has now retrograded; music, supreme at the outset, then neglected, is but now pushing forward into the place which its nature entitles it to occupy. When we conceive of an art-work composed of such elements, and foregoing the adventitious helps which may accrue to it from conventional idioms based on association of ideas, we have before us the concept of Absolute music, whose content, like that of every noble artistic composition, be it of tones or forms or colors or thoughts expressed in words, is that high ideal of goodness, truthfulness, and beauty for which all lofty imaginations strive. Such artworks are the instrumental compositions in the classic forms; such, too, may be said to be the high type of idealized "Programme" music, which, like the "Pastoral" symphony of Beethoven, is designed to awaken emotions like those awakened by the contemplation of things, but does not attempt to depict the things themselves. Having mentioned Programme music I must, of course, try to tell what it is; but the exposition must be preceded by an explanation of a kind of music which, because of its chastity, is set down as the finest form of absolute music. This is Chamber music.

[Sidenote: Chamber music.]

[Sidenote: History of the term.]

[Sidenote: Haydn a servant.]

In a broad sense, but one not employed in modern definition, Chamber music is all music not designed for performance in the church or theatre.

(Out-of-door music cannot be considered among these artistic forms of aristocratic descent.) Once, and indeed at the time of its invention, the term meant music designed especially for the delectation of the most eminent patrons of the art--the kings and nobles whose love for it gave it maintenance and encouragement. This is implied by the term itself, which has the same etymology wherever the form of music is cultivated. In Italian it is Musica da Camera; in French, Musique de Chambre; in German, Kammermusik. All the terms have a common root. The Greek [Greek: kamara] signified an arch, a vaulted room, or a covered wagon. In the time of the Frankish kings the word was applied to the room in the royal palace in which the monarch's private property was kept, and in which he looked after his private affairs. When royalty took up the cultivation of music it was as a private, not as a court, function, and the concerts given for the entertainment of the royal family took place in the king's chamber, or private room. The musicians were nothing more nor less than servants in the royal household. This relationship endured into the present century. Haydn was a Hausofficier of Prince Esterhazy. As vice-chapelmaster he had to appear every morning in the Prince's ante-room to receive orders concerning the dinner-music and other entertainments of the day, and in the certificate of appointment his conduct is regulated with a particularity which we, who remember him and reverence his genius but have forgotten his master, think humiliating in the extreme.

[Sidenote: Beethoven's Chamber music.]

Out of this cultivation of music in the private chamber grew the characteristics of Chamber music, which we must consider if we would enjoy it ourselves and understand the great reverence which the great masters of music have always felt for it. Beethoven was the first great democrat among musicians. He would have none of the shackles which his predecessors wore, and compelled aristocracy of birth to bow to aristocracy of genius. But such was his reverence for the style of music which had grown up in the chambers of the great that he devoted the last three years of his life almost exclusively to its composition; the peroration of his proclamation to mankind consists of his last quartets--the holiest of holy things to the Chamber musicians of to-day.

[Sidenote: The characteristics of Chamber music.]

Chamber music represents pure thought, lofty imagination, and deep learning. These attributes are encouraged by the idea of privacy which is inseparable from the form. Composers find it the finest field for the display of their talents because their own skill in creating is to be paired with trained skill in hearing. Its representative pieces are written for strings alone--trios, quartets, and quintets. With the strings are sometimes associated a pianoforte, or one or more of the solo wind instruments--oboe, clarinet, or French horn; and as a rule the compositions adhere to classical lines (see Chapter V.). Of necessity the modesty of the apparatus compels it to forego nearly all the adventitious helps with which other forms of composition gain public approval. In the delineative arts Chamber music shows analogy with correct drawing and good composition, the absence of which cannot be atoned for by the most gorgeous coloring. In no other style is sympathy between performers and listeners so necessary, and for that reason Chamber music should always be heard in a small room with performers and listeners joined in angelic wedlock. Communities in which it flourishes under such conditions are musical.

[Sidenote: Programme music.]

[Sidenote: The value of superscriptions.]

[Sidenote: The rule of judgment.]

Properly speaking, the term Programme music ought to be applied only to instrumental compositions which make a frank effort to depict scenes, incidents, or emotional processes to which the composer himself gives the clew either by means of a descriptive title or a verbal motto. It is unfortunate that the term has come to be loosely used. In a high sense the purest and best music in the world is programmatic, its programme being, as I have said, that "high ideal of goodness, truthfulness, and beauty" which is the content of all true art. But the origin of the term was vulgar, and the most contemptible piece of tonal imitation now claims kinship in the popular mind with the exquisitely poetical creations of Schumann and the "Pastoral" symphony of Beethoven; and so it is become necessary to defend it in the case of noble compositions. A programme is not necessarily, as Ambros asserts, a certificate of poverty and an admission on the part of the composer that his art has got beyond its natural bounds. Whether it be merely a suggestive title, as in the case of some of the compositions of Beethoven, Schumann, and Mendelssohn, or an extended commentary, as in the symphonic poems of Liszt and the symphonies of Berlioz and Raff, the programme has a distinct value to the composer as well as the hearer. It can make the perceptive sense more impressible to the influence of the music; it can quicken the fancy, and fire the imagination; it can prevent a gross misconception of the intentions of a composer and the character of his composition. Nevertheless, in determining the artistic value of the work, the question goes not to the ingenuity of the programme or the clearness with which its suggestions have been carried out, but to the beauty of the music itself irrespective of the verbal commentary accompanying it. This rule must be maintained in order to prevent a degradation of the object of musical expression. The vile, the ugly, the painful are not fit subjects for music; music renounces, contravenes, negatives itself when it attempts their delineation.

A classification of Programme music might be made on these lines:

[Sidenote: Kinds of Programme music.]

I. Descriptive pieces which rest on imitation or suggestion of natural sounds.

II. Pieces whose contents are purely musical, but the mood of which is suggested by a poetical title.

III. Pieces in which the influence which determined their form and development is indicated not only by a title but also by a motto which is relied upon to mark out a train of thought for the listener which will bring his fancy into union with that of the composer. The motto may be verbal or pictorial.

IV. Symphonies or other composite works which have a title to indicate their general character, supplemented by explanatory superscriptions for each portion.

[Sidenote: Imitation of natural sounds.]

[Sidenote: The nightingale.]

[Sidenote: The cat.]

[Sidenote: The cuckoo.]

The first of these divisions rests upon the employment of the lowest form of conventional musical idiom. The material which the natural world provides for imitation by the musician is exceedingly scant. Unless we descend to mere noise, as in the descriptions of storms and battles (the shrieking of the wind, the crashing of thunder, and the roar of artillery--invaluable aids to the cheap descriptive writer), we have little else than the calls of a few birds. Nearly thirty years ago Wilhelm Tappert wrote an essay which he called "Zooplastik in Tien." He ransacked the musical literature of centuries, but in all his examples the only animals the voices of which are unmistakable are four fowls--the cuckoo, quail (that is the German bird, not the American, which has a different call), the cock, and the hen. He has many descriptive sounds which suggest other birds and beasts, but only by association of idea; separated from title or text they suggest merely what they are--musical phrases. A reiteration of the rhythmical figure called the "Scotch snap," breaking gradually into a trill, is the common symbol of the nightingale's song, but it is not a copy of that song; three or four tones descending chromatically are given as the cat's mew, but they are made to be such only by placing the syllables Mi-au (taken from the vocabulary of the German cat) under them. Instances of this kind might be called characterization, or description by suggestion, and some of the best composers have made use of them, as will appear in these pages presently. The list being so small, and the lesson taught so large, it may be well to give a few striking instances of absolutely imitative music. The first bird to collaborate with a composer seems to have been the cuckoo, whose notes

had sounded in many a folk-song ere Beethoven thought of enlisting the little solo performer in his "Pastoral" symphony. It is to be borne in mind, however, as a fact having some bearing on the artistic value of Programme music, that Beethoven's cuckoo changes his note to please the musician, and, instead of singing a minor third, he sings a major third thus:

[Sidenote: Cock and hen.]

As long ago as 1688 Jacob Walter wrote a musical piece entitled "Gallina et

Gallo," in which the hen was delineated in this theme:

while the cock had the upper voice in the following example, his clear challenge sounding above the cackling of his mate:

The most effective use yet made of the song of the hen, however, is in "La Poule," one of Rameau's "Pies de Clavecin," printed in 1736, a delightful composition with this subject:

[Sidenote: The quail.]

The quail's song is merely a monotonic rhythmical figure to which German fancy has fitted words of pious admonition:

[Sidenote: Conventional idioms.]

[Sidenote: Association of ideas.]

[Sidenote: Fancy and imagination.]

[Sidenote: Harmony and emotionality.]

The paucity of examples in this department is a demonstration of the statement made elsewhere that nature does not provide music with models for imitation as it does painting and sculpture. The fact that, nevertheless, we have come to recognize a large number of idioms based on association of ideas stands the composer in good stead whenever he ventures into the domain of delineative or descriptive music, and this he can do without becoming crudely imitative. Repeated experiences have taught us to recognize resemblances between sequences or combinations of tones and things or ideas, and on these analogies, even though they be purely conventional (that is agreed upon, as we have agreed that a nod of the head shall convey assent, a shake of the head dissent, and a shrug of the shoulders doubt or indifference), the composers have built up a voluminous vocabulary of idioms which need only to be helped out by a suggestion to the mind to be eloquently illustrative. "Sometimes hearing a melody or harmony arouses an emotion like that aroused by the contemplation of a thing. Minor harmonies, slow movements, dark tonal colorings, combine directly to put a musically susceptible person in a mood congenial to thoughts of sorrow and death; and, inversely, the experience of sorrow, or the contemplation of death, creates affinity for minor harmonies, slow movements, and dark tonal colorings. Or we recognize attributes in music possessed also by things, and we consort the music and the things, external attributes bringing descriptive music into play, which excites the fancy, internal attributes calling for an exercise of the loftier faculty, imagination, to discern their meaning."[B] The latter kind is delineative music of the higher order, the kind that I have called idealized programme music, for it is the imagination which, as Ruskin has said, "sees the heart and inner nature and makes them felt, but is often obscure, mysterious, and interrupted in its giving out of outer detail," which is "a seer in the prophetic sense, calling the things that are not as though they were, and forever delighting to dwell on that which is not tangibly present." In this kind of music, harmony, the real seat of emotionality in music, is an eloquent factor, and, indeed, there is no greater mystery in the art, which is full of mystery, than the fact that the lowering of the second tone in the chord, which is the starting-point of harmony, should change an expression of satisfaction, energetic action, or jubilation into an accent of pain or sorrow. The major mode is "to do," the minor, "to suffer:"

[Sidenote: Major and minor.]

[Sidenote: Music and movement.]

How near a large number of suggestions, which are based wholly upon experience or association of ideas, lie to the popular fancy, might be illustrated by scores of examples. Thoughts of religious functions arise in us the moment we hear the trombones intone a solemn phrase in full harmony; an oboe melody in sixth-eighth time over a drone bass brings up a pastoral picture of a shepherd playing upon his pipe; trumpets and drums suggest war, and so on. The delineation of movement is easier to the musician than it is to the poet. Handel, who has conveyed the sensation of a "darkness which might be felt," in a chorus of his "Israel in Egypt," by means which appeal solely to the imagination stirred by feelings, has in the same work pictured the plague of frogs with a frank naivety which almost upsets our seriousness of demeanor, by suggesting the characteristic movement of the creatures in the instrumental accompaniment to the arioso, "Their land brought forth frogs," which begins thus:

[Sidenote: Handel's frogs.]

[Sidenote: The movement of water.]

We find the gentle flux and reflux of water as if it were lapping a rocky shore in the exquisite figure out of which Mendelssohn constructed his "Hebrides" overture:

and in fancy we ride on mighty surges when we listen to the principal subject of Rubinstein's "Ocean" symphony:

In none of these instances can the composer be said to be imitative. Music cannot copy water, but it can do what water does, and so suggest water.

[Sidenote: High and low.]

Some of the most common devices of composers are based on conceptions that are wholly arbitrary. A musical tone cannot have position in space such as is indicated by high or low, yet so familiar is the association of acuteness of pitch with height, and gravity of pitch with depth, that composers continually delineate high things with acute tones and low things with grave tones, as witness Handel in one of the choruses of "The Messiah:"

[Sidenote: Ascent, descent, and distance delineated.]

Similarly, too, does Beethoven describe the ascent into heaven and the descent into hell in the Credo of his mass in D. Beethoven's music, indeed, is full of tone-painting, and because it exemplifies a double device I make room for one more illustration. It is from the cantata "Becalmed at Sea, and a Prosperous Voyage," and in it the composer pictures the immensity of the sea by a sudden, extraordinary spreading out of his harmonies, which is musical, and dwelling a long time on the word "distance" (Weite) which is rhetorical:

[Sidenote: Bald imitation bad art.]

[Sidenote: Vocal music and delineation.]

[Sidenote: Beethoven's canon.]

The extent to which tone-painting is justified is a question which might profitably concern us; but such a discussion as it deserves would far exceed the limits set for this book, and must be foregone. It cannot be too forcibly urged, however, as an aid to the listener, that efforts at musical cartooning have never been made by true composers, and that in the degree that music attempts simply to copy external things it falls in the scale of artistic truthfulness and value. Vocal music tolerates more of the descriptive element than instrumental because it is a mixed art; in it the purpose of music is to illustrate the poetry and, by intensifying the appeal to the fancy, to warm the emotions. Every piece of vocal music, moreover, carries its explanatory programme in its words. Still more tolerable and even righteous is it in the opera where it is but one of several factors which labor together to make up the sum of dramatic representation. But it must ever remain valueless unless it be idealized. Mendelssohn, desiring to put Bully Bottom into the overture to "A Midsummer Night's Dream," did not hesitate to use tones which suggest the bray of a donkey, yet the effect, like Handel's frogs and flies in "Israel," is one of absolute musical value. The canon which ought continually to be before the mind of the listener is that which Beethoven laid down with most painstaking care when he wrote the "Pastoral" symphony. Desiring to inform the listeners what were the images which inspired the various movements (in order, of course, that they might the better enter into the work by recalling them), he gave each part a superscription thus:

[Sidenote: The "Pastoral" symphony.]

I. "The agreeable and cheerful sensations awakened by arrival in the country."

II. "Scene by the brook."

III. "A merrymaking of the country folk."

IV. "Thunder-storm."

V. "Shepherds' song--feelings of charity combined with gratitude to the Deity after the storm."

In the title itself he included an admonitory explanation which should have everlasting validity: "Pastoral Symphony; more expression of feeling than painting." How seriously he thought on the subject we know from his sketch-books, in which occur a number of notes, some of which were evidently hints for superscriptions, some records of his convictions on the subject of descriptive music. The notes are reprinted in Nottebohm's "Zweite Beethoveniana," but I borrow Sir George Grove's translation:

[Sidenote: Beethoven's notes on descriptive music.]

"The hearers should be allowed to discover the situations."

"Sinfonia caracteristica, or a recollection of country life."

"All painting in instrumental music, if pushed too far, is a failure."

"Sinfonia pastorella. Anyone who has an idea of country life can make out for himself the intentions of the author without many titles."

"People will not require titles to recognize the general intention to be more a matter of feeling than of painting in sounds."

"Pastoral symphony: No picture, but something in which the emotions are expressed which are aroused in men by the pleasure of the country (or), in which some feelings of country life are set forth."[C]

As to the relation of programme to music Schumann laid down an admirable maxim when he said that while good music was not harmed by a descriptive title it was a bad indication if a composition needed one.

[Sidenote: Classic and Romantic.]

There are, among all the terms used in music, no words of vaguer meaning than Classic and Romantic. The idea which they convey most widely in conjunction is that of antithesis. When the Romantic School of composers is discussed it is almost universally presented as something opposed in character to the Classical School. There is little harm in this if we but bear in mind that all the terms which have come into use to describe different phases of musical development are entirely artificial and arbitrary--that they do not stand for anything absolute, but only serve as platforms of observation. If the terms had a fixed meaning we ought to be able, since they have established themselves in the language of history and criticism, to describe unambiguously and define clearly the boundary which separates them. This, however, is impossible. Each generation, nay, each decade, fixes the meaning of the words for itself and decides what works shall go into each category. It ought to be possible to discover a principle, a touchstone, which shall emancipate us from the mischievous and misleading notions that have so long prompted men to make the partitions between the schools out of dates and names.

[Sidenote: Trench's definition of "classical."]

The terms were borrowed from literary criticism; but even there, in the words of Archbishop Trench, "they either say nothing at all or say something erroneous." Classical has more to defend it than Romantic, because it has greater antiquity and, in one sense, has been used with less arbitrariness.

"The term," says Trench, "is drawn from the political economy of Rome. Such a man was rated as to his income in the third class, such another in the fourth, and so on, and he who was in the highest was emphatically said to be of the class, classicus, a class man, without adding the number as in that case superfluous; while all others were _infra classem_. Hence by an obvious analogy the best authors were rated as classici, or men of the highest class; just as in English we say 'men of rank' absolutely for men who are in the highest ranks of the State."

Thus Trench, and his historical definition, explains why in music also there is something more than a lurking suggestion of excellence in the conception of "classical;" but that fact does not put away the quarrel which we feel exists between Classic and Romantic.

[Sidenote: Romantic in literature.]

[Sidenote: Schumann and Jean Paul.]

[Sidenote: Weber's operas.]

[Sidenote: Mendelssohn.]

As applied to literature Romantic was an adjective affected by certain poets, first in Germany, then in France, who wished to introduce a style of thought and expression different from that of those who followed old models. Intrinsically, of course, the term does not imply any such opposition but only bears witness to the source from which the poets drew their inspiration. This was the imaginative literature of the Middle Ages, the fantastical stories of chivalry and knighthood written in the Romance, or Romanic languages, such as Italian, Spanish, and Provencial. The principal elements of these stories were the marvellous and the supernatural. The composers whose names first spring into our minds when we think of the Romantic School are men like Mendelssohn and Schumann, who drew much of their inspiration from the young writers of their time who were making war on stilted rhetoric and conventionalism of phrase. Schumann touches hands with the Romantic poets in their strivings in two directions. His artistic conduct, especially in his early years, is inexplicable if Jean Paul be omitted from the equation. His music rebels against the formalism which had held despotic sway over the art, and also seeks to disclose the beauty which lies buried in the world of mystery in and around us, and give expression to the multitude of emotions to which unyielding formalism had refused adequate utterance. This, I think, is the chief element of Romanticism. Another has more of an external nature and genesis, and this we find in the works of such composers as Von Weber, who is Romantic chiefly in his operas, because of the supernaturalism and chivalry in their stories, and Mendelssohn, who, while distinctly Romantic in many of his strivings, was yet so great a master of form, and so attached to it, that the Romantic side of him was not fully developed.

[Sidenote: A definition of "Classical" in music.]

[Sidenote: The creative and conservative principles.]

[Sidenote: Musical laws of necessity progressive.]

[Sidenote: Bach and Romanticism.]

[Sidenote: Creation and conservation.]

If I were to attempt a definition it would be this: Classical composers are those of the first rank (to this extent we yield to the ancient Roman conception) who have developed music to the highest pitch of perfection on its formal side and, in obedience to generally accepted laws, preferring aesthetic beauty, pure and simple, over emotional content, or, at any rate, refusing to sacrifice form to characteristic expression. Romantic composers are those who have sought their ideals in other regions and striven to give expression to them irrespective of the restrictions and limitations of form and the conventions of law--composers with whom, in brief, content outweighs manner. This definition presents Classicism as the regulative and conservative principle in the history of the art, and Romanticism as the progressive, regenerative, and creative principle. It is easy to see how the notion of contest between them grew up, and the only harm which can come from such a notion will ensue only if we shut our eyes to the fact that it is a contest between two elements whose very opposition stimulates life, and whose union, perfect, peaceful, mutually supplemental, is found in every really great art-work. No law which fixes, and hence limits, form, can remain valid forever. Its end is served when it enforces itself long enough to keep lawlessness in check till the test of time has determined what is sound, sweet, and wholesome in the innovations which are always crowding eagerly into every creative activity in art and science. In art it is ever true, as Faust concludes, that "In the beginning was the deed." The laws of composition are the products of compositions; and, being such, they cannot remain unalterable so long as the impulse freshly to create remains. All great men are ahead of their time, and in all great music, no matter when written, you shall find instances of profounder meaning and deeper or newer feeling than marked the generality of contemporary compositions. So Bach frequently floods his formal utterances with Romantic feeling, and the face of Beethoven, serving at the altar in the temple of Beauty, is transfigured for us by divine light. The principles of creation and conservation move onward together, and what is Romantic to-day becomes Classic to-morrow. Romanticism is fluid Classicism. It is the emotional stimulus informing Romanticism which calls music into life, but no sooner is it born, free, untrammelled, nature's child, than the regulative principle places shackles upon it; but it is enslaved only that it may become and remain art.

FOOTNOTES:

[B] "Studies in the Wagnerian Drama," p. 22.

[C] "Beethoven and His Nine Symphonies," by George Grove, C.B., 2d ed., p. 191.

IV

The Modern Orchestra

[Sidenote: The orchestra as an instrument.]

[Sidenote: What may be heard from a band.]

The most eloquent, potent, and capable instrument of music in the world is the modern orchestra. It is the instrument whose employment by the classical composers and the geniuses of the Romantic School in the middle of our century marks the high tide of the musical art. It is an instrument, moreover, which is never played upon without giving a great object-lesson in musical analysis, without inviting the eye to help the ear to discern the cause of the sounds which ravish our senses and stir up pleasurable emotions. Yet the popular knowledge of its constituent parts, of the individual value and mission of the factors which go to make up its sum, is scarcely greater than the popular knowledge of the structure of a symphony or sonata. All this is the more deplorable since at least a rudimentary knowledge of these things might easily be gained, and in gaining it the student would find a unique intellectual enjoyment, and have his ears unconsciously opened to a thousand beauties in the music never perceived before. He would learn, for instance, to distinguish the characteristic timbre of each of the instruments in the band; and after that to the delight found in what may be called the primary colors he would add that which comes from analyzing the vast number of tints which are the products of combination. Noting the capacity of the various instruments and the manner in which they are employed, he would get glimpses into the mental workshop of the composer. He would discover that there are conventional means of expression in his art analogous to those in the other arts; and collating his methods with the effects produced, he would learn something of the creative artist's purposes. He would find that while his merely sensuous enjoyment would be left unimpaired, and the emotional excitement which is a legitimate fruit of musical performance unchecked, these pleasures would have others consorted with them. His intellectual faculties would be agreeably excited, and he would enjoy the pleasures of memory, which are exemplified in music more delightfully and more frequently than in any other art, because of the role which repetition of parts plays in musical composition.

[Sidenote: Familiar instruments.]

[Sidenote: The instrumental choirs.]

The argument is as valid in the study of musical forms as in the study of the orchestra, but it is the latter that is our particular business in this chapter. Everybody listening to an orchestral concert recognizes the physical forms of the violins, flutes, cornets, and big drum; but even of these familiar instruments the voices are not always recognized. As for the rest of the harmonious fraternity, few give heed to them, even while enjoying the music which they produce; yet with a few words of direction anybody can study the instruments of the band at an orchestral concert. Let him first recognize the fact that to the mind of a composer an orchestra always presents itself as a combination of four groups of instruments--choirs, let us call them, with unwilling apology to the lexicographers. These choirs are: first, the viols of four sorts--violins, violas, violoncellos, and double-basses, spoken of collectively as the "string quartet;" second, the wind instruments of wood (the "wood-winds" in the musician's jargon)--flutes, oboes, clarinets, and bassoons; third, the wind instruments of brass (the "brass")--trumpets, horns, trombones, and bass tuba. In all of these subdivisions there are numerous variations which need not detain us now. A further subdivision might be made in each with reference to the harmony voices (showing an analogy with the four voices of a vocal choir--soprano, contralto, tenor, and bass); but to go into this might make the exposition confusing. The fourth "choir" (here the apology to the lexicographers must be repeated with much humility and earnestness) consists of the instruments of percussion--the kettle-drums, big drum, cymbals, triangle, bell chime, etc. (sometimes spoken of collectively in the United States as "the battery").

[Illustration: SEATING PLAN OF THE NEW YORK PHILHARMONIC SOCIETY.]

[Sidenote: How orchestras are seated.]

[Sidenote: Plan of the New York Philharmonic.]

The disposition of these instruments in our orchestras is largely a matter of individual taste and judgment in the conductor, though the general rule is exemplified in the plan given herewith, showing how Mr. Anton Seidl has arranged the desks for the concerts of the Philharmonic Society of New York. Mr. Theodore Thomas's arrangement differed very little from that of Mr. Seidl, the most noticeable difference being that he placed the viola-players beside the second violinists, where Mr. Seidl has the violoncellists. Mr. Seidl's purpose in making the change was to gain an increase in sonority for the viola part, the position to the right of the stage (the left of the audience) enabling the viola-players to hold their instruments with the F-holes toward the listeners instead of away from them. The relative positions of the harmonious battalions, as a rule, are as shown in the diagram. In the foreground, the violins, violas, and 'cellos; in the middle distance, the wood-winds; in the background, the brass and the battery; the double-basses flanking the whole body. This distribution of forces is dictated by considerations of sonority, the most assertive instruments--the brass and drums--being placed farthest from the hearers, and the instruments of the viol tribe, which are the real backbone of the band and make their effect by a massing of voices in each part, having the place of honor and greatest advantage. Of course it is understood that I am speaking of a concert orchestra. In the case of theatrical or operatic bands the arrangement of the forces is dependent largely upon the exigencies of space.

[Sidenote: Solo instruments.]

Outside the strings the instruments are treated by composers as solo instruments, a single flute, oboe, clarinet, or other wind instrument sometimes doing the same work in the development of the composition as the entire body of first violins. As a rule, the wood-winds are used in pairs, the purpose of this being either to fill the harmony when what I may call the principal thought of the composition is consigned to a particular choir, or to strengthen a voice by permitting two instruments to play in unison.

[Sidenote: Groupings for harmony effects.]

[Sidenote: Wagner's instrumental characterization.]

[Sidenote: An instrumental language.]

Each choir, except the percussion instruments, is capable of playing in full harmony; and this effect is frequently used by composers. In "Lohengrin," which for that reason affords to the amateur an admirable opportunity for orchestral study, Wagner resorts to this device in some instances for the sake of dramatic characterization. Elsa, a dreamy, melancholy maiden, crushed under the weight of wrongful accusation, and sustained only by the vision of a seraphic champion sent by Heaven to espouse her cause, is accompanied on her entrance and sustained all through her scene of trial by the dulcet tones of the wood-winds, the oboe most often carrying the melody. Lohengrin's superterrestrial character as a Knight of the Holy Grail is prefigured in the harmonies which seem to stream from the violins, and in the prelude tell of the bringing of the sacred vessel of Christ's passion to Monsalvat; but in his chivalric character he is greeted by the militant trumpets in a strain of brilliant puissance and rhythmic energy. Composers have studied the voices of the instruments so long and well, and have noted the kind of melodies and harmonies in which the voices are most effective, that they have formulated what might almost be called an instrumental language. Though the effective capacity of each instrument is restricted not only by its mechanics, but also by the quality of its tones--a melody conceived for one instrument sometimes becoming utterly inexpressive and unbeautiful by transferrence to another--the range of effects is extended almost to infinity by means of combination, or, as a painter might say, by mixing the colors. The art of writing effectively for instruments in combination is the art of instrumentation or orchestration, in which Berlioz and Wagner were Past Grand Masters.

[Sidenote: Number of instruments.]

The number of instruments of each kind in an orchestra may also be said to depend measurably upon the music, or the use to which the band is to be put. Neither in instruments nor in numbers is there absolute identity between a dramatic and a symphonic orchestra. The apparatus of the former is generally much more varied and complex, because of the vast development of variety in dramatic expression stimulated by Wagner.

[Sidenote: Symphony and dramatic orchestras.]

The modern symphony, especially the symphonic poem, shows the influence of this dramatic tendency, but not in the same degree. A comparison between model bands in each department will disclose what is called the normal orchestral organization. For the comparison (see page 82), I select the bands of the first Wagner Festival held in Bayreuth in 1876, the Philharmonic Society of New York, the Boston Symphony Orchestra, and the Chicago Symphony Orchestra.

[Sidenote: Instruments rarely used.]

Instruments like the corno di bassetto, bass trumpet, tenor tuba, contra-bass tuba, and contra-bass trombone are so seldom called for in the music played by concert orchestras that they have no place in their regular lists. They are employed when needed, however, and the horns and other instruments are multiplied when desirable effects are to be obtained by such means.

[Sidenote: Orchestras compared.]

Instruments	Bayreuth	New York Philharmonic	Boston	Chicago
First violins	16	18	16	16
Second violins	16	18	14	16
Violas	12	14	10	10
Violoncellos	12	14	8	10
Double-basses	8	14	8	9
Flutes	3	3	3	3
Oboes	3	3	2	3
English horn	1	1	1	1
Clarinets	3	3	3	3
Basset-horn	1	0	0	0
Bassoons	3	3	3	3
Trumpets or cornets	3	3	4	4
Horns	8	4	4	4
Trombones	3	3	3	3
Bass trumpet	1	0	0	1
Tenor tubas	2	0	2	4
Bass tubas	2	1	2	1
Contra-bass tuba	1	0	1	0
Contra-bass trombone	1	0	0	1
Tympani (pairs)	2	2	2	2
Bass drum	1	1	1	1
Cymbals (pairs)	1	1	1	1
Harps	6	1	1	2

[Sidenote: The string quartet.]

[Sidenote: Old laws against instrumentalists.]

[Sidenote: Early instrumentation.]

[Sidenote: Handel's orchestra.]

The string quartet, it will be seen, makes up nearly three-fourths of a well-balanced orchestra. It is the only choir which has numerous representation of its constituent units. This was not always so, but is the fruit of development in the art of instrumentation which is the newest department in music. Vocal music had reached its highest point before instrumental music made a beginning as an art. The former was the pampered child of the Church, the latter was long an outlaw. As late as the fourteenth and fifteenth centuries instrumentalists were vagabonds in law, like strolling players. They had none of the rights of citizenship; the religious sacraments were denied them; their children were not permitted to inherit property or learn an honourable trade; and after death the property for which they had toiled escheated to the crown. After the instruments had achieved the privilege of artistic utterance, they were for a long time mere slavish imitators of the human voice. Bach treated them with an insight into their possibilities which was far in advance of his time, for which reason he is the most modern composer of the first half of the eighteenth century; but even in Handel's case the rule was to treat them chiefly as supports for the voices. He multiplied them just as he did the voices in his choruses, consorting a choir of oboes and bassoons, and another of trumpets of almost equal numbers with his violins.

[Sidenote: The modern band.]

The so-called purists in England talk a great deal about restoring Handel's orchestra in performances of his oratorios, utterly unmindful of the fact that to our ears, accustomed to the myriad-hued orchestra of to-day, the effect would seem opaque, heavy, unbalanced, and without charm were a band of oboes to play in unison with the violins, another of bassoons to double the 'cellos, and half a dozen trumpets to come flaring and crashing into the musical mass at intervals. Gluck in the opera, and Haydn and Mozart in the symphony, first disclosed the charm of the modern orchestra with the wind instruments apportioned to the strings so as to obtain the multitude of tonal tints which we admire to-day. On the lines which they marked out the progress has been exceedingly rapid and far-reaching.

[Sidenote: Capacity of the orchestra.]

[Sidenote: The extremes of range.]

In the hands of the latter-day Romantic composers, and with the help of the instrument-makers, who have marvellously increased the capacity of the wind instruments, and remedied the deficiencies which embarrassed the Classical writers, the orchestra has developed into an instrument such as never entered the mind of the wildest dreamer of the last century. Its range of expression is almost infinite. It can strike like a thunder-bolt, or murmur like a zephyr. Its voices are multitudinous. Its register is coextensive in theory with that of the modern pianoforte, reaching from the space immediately below the sixth added line under the bass staff to the ninth added line above the treble staff. These two extremes, which belong respectively to the bass tuba and piccolo flute, are not at the command of every player, but they are within the capacity of the instruments, and mark the orchestra's boundaries in respect of pitch. The gravest note is almost as deep as any in which the ordinary human ear can detect pitch, and the acutest reaches the same extremity in the opposite direction.

[Sidenote: The viols.]

[Sidenote: The violin.]

With all the changes that have come over the orchestra in the course of the last two hundred years, the string quartet has remained its chief factor. Its voice cannot grow monotonous or cloying, for, besides its innate qualities, it commands a more varied manner of expression than all the other instruments combined. The viol, which term I shall use generically to indicate all the instruments of the quartet, is the only instrument in the band, except the harp, that can play harmony as well as melody. Its range is the most extensive; it is more responsive to changes in manipulation; it is endowed more richly than any other instrument with varieties of timbre; it has an incomparable facility of execution, and answers more quickly and more eloquently than any of its companions to the feelings of the player. A great advantage which the viol possesses over wind instruments is that, not being dependent on the breath of the player, there is practically no limit to its ability to sustain tones. It is because of this long list of good qualities that it is relied on to provide the staff of life to instrumental music. The strings as commonly used show four members of the viol family, distinguished among themselves by their size, and the quality in the changes of tone which grows out of the differences in size. The violins (Appendix, Plate I.) are the smallest members of the family. Historically they are the culmination of a development toward diminutiveness, for in their early days viols were larger than they are now. When the violin of to-day entered the orchestra (in the score of Monteverde's opera "Orfeo") it was specifically described as a "little French violin." Its voice, Berlioz says, is the "true female voice of the orchestra." Generally the violin part of an orchestral score is two-voiced, but the two groups may be split into a great number. In one passage in "Tristan und Isolde" Wagner divides his first and second violins into sixteen groups. Such divisions, especially in the higher regions, are productive of entrancing effects.

[Sidenote: Violin effects.]

[Sidenote: Pizzicato.]

[Sidenote: "Col legno dall'arco."]

[Sidenote: Harmonics.]

[Sidenote: Vibrato.]

[Sidenote: "Con sordino."]

The halo of sound which streams from the beginning and end of the "Lohengrin" prelude is produced by this device. High and close harmonies from divided violins always sound ethereal. Besides their native tone quality (that resulting from a string stretched over a sounding shell set to vibrating by friction), the violins have a number of modified qualities resulting from changes in manipulation. Sometimes the strings are plucked (pizzicato), when the result is a short tone something like that of a banjo with the metallic clang omitted; very dainty effects can thus be produced, and though it always seems like a degradation of the instrument so pre-eminently suited to a broad singing style, no less significant a symphonist than Tschaikowsky has written a Scherzo in which the violins are played pizzicato throughout the movement. Ballet composers frequently resort to the piquant effect, but in the larger and more serious forms of composition, the device is sparingly used. Differences in quality and expressiveness of tone are also produced by varied methods of applying the bow to the strings: with stronger or lighter pressure; near the bridge, which renders the tone hard and brilliant, and over the end of the finger-board, which softens it; in a continuous manner (legato), or detached (staccato). Weird effects in dramatic music are sometimes produced by striking the strings with the wood of the bow, Wagner resorting to this means to delineate the wicked glee of his dwarf Mime, and Meyerbeer to heighten the uncanniness of Nelusko's wild song in the third act of "L'Africaine." Another class of effects results from the manner in which the strings are "stopped" by the fingers of the left hand. When they are not pressed firmly against the finger-board but touched lightly at certain places called nodes by the acousticians, so that the segments below the finger are permitted to vibrate along with the upper portion, those peculiar tones of a flute-like quality called harmonics or flageolet tones are produced. These are oftener heard in dramatic music than in symphonies; but Berlioz, desiring to put Shakespeare's description of Queen Mab,

"Her wagon-spokes made of long spinner's legs; The cover, of the wings of grasshoppers; The traces, of the smallest spider's web; The collars, of the moonshine's watery beams--"

into music in his dramatic symphony, "Romeo and Juliet," achieved a marvellously filmy effect by dividing his violins, and permitting some of them to play harmonics. Yet so little was his ingenious purpose suspected when he first brought the symphony forward in Paris, that one of the critics spoke contemptuously of this effect as sounding "like an ill-greased syringe." A quivering motion imparted to the fingers of the left hand in stopping the strings produces a tremulousness of tone akin to the vibrato of a singer; and, like the vocal vibrato, when not carried to excess, this effect is a potent expression of sentimental feeling. But it is much abused by solo players. Another modification of tone is caused by placing a tiny instrument called a sordino, or mute, upon the bridge. This clamps the bridge, makes it heavier, and checks the vibrations, so that the tone is muted or muffled, and at times sounds mysterious.

[Sidenote: Pizzicato on the basses.]

[Sidenote: Tremolo.]

These devices, though as a rule they have their maximum of effectiveness in the violins, are possible also on the violas, violoncellos, and double-basses, which, as I have already intimated, are but violins of a larger growth. The pizzicato is, indeed, oftenest heard from the double-basses, where it has a much greater eloquence than on the violins. In music of a sombre cast, the short, deep tones given out by the plucked strings of the contra-bass sometimes have the awfulness of gigantic heart-throbs. The difficulty of producing the other effects grows with the increase of difficulty in handling the instruments, this being due to the growing thickness of the strings and the wideness of the points at which they must be stopped. One effect peculiar to them all--the most used of all effects, indeed, in dramatic music--is the tremolo, produced by dividing a tone into many quickly reiterated short tones by a rapid motion of the bow. This device came into use with one of the earliest pieces of dramatic music. It is two centuries old, and was first used to help in the musical delineation of a combat. With scarcely an exception, the varied means which I have described can be detected by those to whom they are not already familiar by watching the players while listening to the music.

[Sidenote: The viola.]

The viola is next in size to the violin, and is tuned at the interval of a fifth lower. Its highest string is A, which is the second string of the violin, and its lowest C. Its tone, which sometimes contains a comical suggestion of a boy's voice in mutation, is lacking in incisiveness and brilliancy, but for this it compensates by a wonderful richness and filling quality, and a pathetic and inimitable mournfulness in melancholy music. It blends beautifully with the violoncello, and is often made to double that instrument's part for the sake of color effect--as, to cite a familiar instance, in the principal subject of the Andante in Beethoven's Fifth Symphony.

[Sidenote: The violoncello.]

[Sidenote: Violoncello effects.]

The strings of the violoncello (Plate II.) are tuned like those of the viola, but an octave lower. It is the knee-fiddle (_viola da gamba) of the last century, as the viola is the arm-fiddle (viola da braccio_), and got its old name from the position in which it is held by the player. The 'cello's voice is a bass--it might be called the barytone of the choir--and in the olden time of simple writing, little else was done with it than to double the bass part one octave higher. But modern composers, appreciating its marvellous capacity for expression, which is next to that of the violin, have treated it with great freedom and independence as a solo instrument. Its tone is full of voluptuous languor. It is the sighing lover of the instrumental company, and can speak the language of tender passion more feelingly than any of its fellows. The ravishing effect of a multiplication of its voice is tellingly exemplified in the opening of the overture to "William Tell," which is written for five solo 'celli, though it is oftenest heard in an arrangement which gives two of the middle parts to violas. When Beethoven wished to produce the emotional impression of a peacefully rippling brook in his "Pastoral" symphony, he gave a murmuring figure to the divided violoncellos, and Wagner uses the passionate accents of four of these instruments playing in harmony to support Siegmund when he is pouring out the ecstasy of his love in the first act of "Die Walke." In the love scene of Berlioz's "Romeo and Juliet" symphony it is the violoncello which personifies the lover, and holds converse with the modest oboe.

[Sidenote: The double-bass.]

The patriarchal double-bass is known to all, and also its mission of providing the foundation for the harmonic structure of orchestral music. It sounds an octave lower than the music written for it, being what is called a transposing instrument of sixteen-foot tone. Solos are seldom written for this instrument in orchestral music, though Beethoven, with his daring recitatives in the Ninth Symphony, makes it a mediator between the instrumental and vocal forces. Dragonetti and Bottesini, two Italians, the latter of whom is still alive, won great fame as solo players on the unwieldy instrument. The latter uses a small bass viol, and strings it with harp strings; but Dragonetti played a full double-bass, on which he could execute the most difficult passages written for the violoncello.

[Sidenote: The wood-winds.]

Since the instruments of the wood-wind choir are frequently used in solos, their acquaintance can easily be made by an observing amateur. To this division of the orchestra belong the gentle accents in the instrumental language. Violent expression is not its province, and generally when the band is discoursing in heroic style or giving voice to brave or angry emotion the wood-winds are either silent or are used to give weight to the body of tone rather than color. Each of the instruments has a strongly characteristic voice, which adapts itself best to a certain style of music; but by use of different registers and by combinations among them, or with the instruments of the other choirs, a wide range of expression within the limits suggested has been won for the wood-winds.

[Sidenote: The flute.]

[Sidenote: The piccolo flute.]

[Sidenote: Janizary music.]

[Sidenote: The story of the flute.]

The flute, which requires no description, is, for instance, an essentially soulless instrument; but its marvellous agility and the effectiveness with which its tones can be blended with others make it one of the most useful instruments in the band. Its native character, heard in the compositions written for it as a solo instrument, has prevented it from being looked upon with dignity. As a rule, brilliancy is all that is expected from it. It is a sort of _soprano leggiero_ with a small range of superficial feelings. It can sentimentalize, and, as Dryden says, be "soft, complaining," but when we hear it pour forth a veritable ecstasy of jubilation, as it does in the dramatic climax of Beethoven's overture "Leonore No. 3," we marvel at the transformation effected by the composer. Advantage has also been taken of the difference between its high and low tones, and now in some romantic music, as in Raff's "Lenore" symphony, or the prayer of Agathe in "Der Freischez," the hollowness of the low tones produces a mysterious effect that is exceedingly striking. Still the fact remains that the native voice of the instrument, though sweet, is expressionless compared with that of the oboe or clarinet. Modern composers sometimes write for three flutes; but in the older writers, when a third flute is used, it is generally an octave flute, or piccolo flute (Plate III.)--a tiny instrument whose aggressiveness of voice is out of all proportion to its diminutiveness of body. This is the instrument which shrieks and whistles when the band is playing at storm-making, to imitate the noise of the wind. It sounds an octave higher than is indicated by the notes in its part, and so is what is called a transposing instrument of four-foot tone. It revels in military music, which is proper, for it is an own cousin to the ear-piercing fife, which annually makes up for its long silence in the noisy days before political elections. When you hear a composition in march time, with bass and snare drum, cymbals and triangle, such as the Germans call "Turkish" or "Janizary" music, you may be sure to hear also the piccolo flute. The flute is doubtless one of the oldest instruments in the world. The primitive cave-dwellers made flutes of the leg-bones of birds and other animals, an origin of which a record is preserved in the Latin name tibia. The first wooden flutes were doubtless the Pandean pipes, in which the tone was produced by blowing across the open ends of hollow reeds. The present method, already known to the ancient Egyptians, of closing the upper end, and creating the tone by blowing across a hole cut in the side, is only a modification of the method pursued, according to classic tradition, by Pan when he breathed out his dejection at the loss of the nymph Syrinx, by blowing across the tuneful reeds which were that nymph in her metamorphosed state.

[Sidenote: Reed instruments.]

[Sidenote: Double reeds.]

The flute or pipe of the Greeks and Romans was only distantly related to the true flute, but was the ancestor of its orchestral companions, the oboe and clarinet. These instruments are sounded by being blown in at the end, and the tone is created by vibrating reeds, whereas in the flute it is the result of the impinging of the air on the edge of the hole called the embouchure, and the consequent stirring of the column of air in the flue of the instrument. The reeds are thin slips or blades of cane. The size and bore of the instruments and the difference between these reeds are the causes of the differences in tone quality between these relatives. The oboe or hautboy, English horn, and the bassoon have what are called double reeds. Two narrow blades of cane are fitted closely together, and fastened with silk on a small metal tube extending from the upper end of the instrument in the case of the oboe and English horn, from the side in the case of the bassoon. The reeds are pinched more or less tightly between the lips, and are set to vibrating by the breath.

[Sidenote: The oboe.]

[Sidenote: The English horn.]

The oboe (Plate IV.) is naturally associated with music of a pastoral character. It is pre-eminently a melody instrument, and though its voice comes forth shrinkingly, its uniqueness of tone makes it easily heard. It is a most lovable instrument. "Candor, artless grace, soft joy, or the grief of a fragile being suits the oboe's accents," says Berlioz. The peculiarity of its mouth-piece gives its tone a reedy or vibrating quality totally unlike the clarinet's. Its natural alto is the English horn (Plate V.), which is an oboe of larger growth, with curved tube for convenience of manipulation. The tone of the English horn is fuller, nobler, and is very attractive in melancholy or dreamy music. There are few players on the English horn in this country, and it might be set down as a rule that outside of New York, Boston, and Chicago, the English horn parts are played by the oboe in America. No melody displays the true character of the English horn better than the Ranz des Vaches in the overture to Rossini's "William Tell"--that lovely Alpine song which the flute embroiders with exquisite ornament. One of the noblest utterances of the oboe is the melody of the funeral march in Beethoven's "Heroic" symphony, in which its tenderness has beautiful play. It is sometimes used effectively in imitative music. In Haydn's "Seasons," and also in that grotesque tone poem by Saint-Sas, the "Danse Macabre," it gives the cock crow. It is the timid oboe that sounds the A for the orchestra to tune by.

[Sidenote: The bassoon.]

[Sidenote: An orchestral humorist.]

[Sidenote: Supernatural effects.]

The grave voice of the oboe is heard from the bassoon (Plate VI.), where, without becoming assertive, it gains a quality entirely unknown to the oboe and English horn. It is this quality that makes the bassoon the humorist par excellence of the orchestra. It is a reedy bass, very apt to recall to those who have had a country education the squalling tone of the homely instrument which the farmer's boy fashions out of the stems of the pumpkin-vine. The humor of the bassoon is an unconscious humor, and results from the use made of its abysmally solemn voice. This solemnity in quality is paired with astonishing flexibility of utterance, so that its gambols are always grotesque. Brahms permits the bassoon to intone the Fuchslied of the German students in his "Academic" overture. Beethoven achieves a decidedly comical effect by a stubborn reiteration of key-note, fifth, and octave by the bassoon under a rustic dance intoned by the oboe in the scherzo of his "Pastoral" symphony; and nearly every modern composer has taken advantage of the instrument's grotesqueness. Mendelssohn introduces the clowns in his "Midsummer-Night's-Dream" music by a droll dance for two bassoons over a sustained bass note from the violoncellos; but when Meyerbeer wanted a very different effect, a ghastly one indeed, in the scene of the resuscitation of the nuns in his "Robert le Diable," he got it by taking two bassoons as solo instruments and using their weak middle tones, which, Berlioz says, have "a pale, cold, cadaverous sound." Singularly enough, Handel resorted to a similar device in his "Saul," to accompany the vision of the Witch of Endor.

[Sidenote: The double bassoon.]

In all these cases a great deal depends upon the relation between the character of the melody and the nature of the instrument to which it is set. A swelling martial fanfare may be made absurd by changing it from trumpets to a weak-voiced wood-wind. It is only the string quartet that speaks all the musical languages of passion and emotion. The double-bassoon is so large an instrument that it has to be bent on itself to bring it under the control of the player. It sounds an octave lower than the written notes. It is not brought often into the orchestra, but speaks very much to the purpose in Brahms's beautiful variations on a theme by Haydn, and the glorious finale of Beethoven's Fifth Symphony.

[Sidenote: The clarinet.]

[Sidenote: The bass clarinet.]

The clarinet (Plate VII.) is the most eloquent member of the wood-wind choir, and, except some of its own modifications or the modifications of the oboe and bassoon, the latest arrival in the harmonious company. It is only a little more than a century old. It has the widest range of expression of the wood-winds, and its chief structural difference is in its mouth-piece. It has a single flat reed, which is much wider than that of the oboe or bassoon, and is fastened by a metallic band and screw to the flattened side of the mouth-piece, whose other side is cut down, chisel shape, for convenience. Its voice is rich, mellow, less reedy, and much fuller and more limpid than the voice of the oboe, which Berlioz tries to describe by analogy as "sweet-sour." It is very flexible, too, and has a range of over three and a half octaves. Its high tones are sometimes shrieky, however, and the full beauty of the instrument is only disclosed when it sings in the middle register. Every symphony and overture contains passages for the clarinet which serve to display its characteristics. Clarinets are made of different sizes for different keys, the smallest being that in E-flat, with an unpleasantly piercing tone, whose use is confined to military bands. There is also an alto clarinet and a bass clarinet (Plate VIII.). The bell of the latter instrument is bent upward, pipe fashion, and its voice is peculiarly impressive and noble. It is a favorite solo instrument in Liszt's symphonic poems.

[Sidenote: Lips and reeds.]

[Sidenote: The brass instruments.]

[Sidenote: Improvements in brass instruments.]

[Sidenote: Valves and slides.]

The fundamental principle of the instruments last described is the production of tone by vibrating reeds. In the instruments of the brass choir, the duty of the reeds is performed by the lips of the player. Variety of tone in respect of quality is produced by variations in size, shape, and modifications in parts like the bell and mouth-piece. The forte of the orchestra receives the bulk of its puissance from the brass instruments, which, nevertheless, can give voice to an extensive gamut of sentiments and feelings. There is nothing more cheery and jocund than the flourishes of the horns, but also nothing more mild and soothing than the songs which sometimes they sing. There is nothing more solemn and religious than the harmony of the trombones, while "the trumpet's loud clangor" is the very voice of a war-like spirit. All of these instruments have undergone important changes within the last few score years. The classical composers, almost down to our own time, were restricted in the use of them because they were merely natural tubes, and their notes were limited to the notes which inflexible tubes can produce. Within this century, however, they have all been transformed from imperfect diatonic instruments to perfect chromatic instruments; that is to say, every brass instrument which is in use now can give out all the semitones within its compass. This has been accomplished through the agency of valves, by means of which differing lengths of the sonorous tube are brought within the command of the players. In the case of the trombones an exceedingly venerable means of accomplishing the same end is applied. The tube is in part made double, one part sliding over the other. By moving his arm, the player lengthens or shortens the tube, and thus changing the key of the instrument, acquires all the tones which can be obtained from so many tubes of different lengths. The mouth-pieces of the trumpet, trombone, and tuba are cup-shaped, and larger than the mouth-piece of the horn, which is little else than a flare of the slender tube, sufficiently wide to receive enough of the player's lips to form the embouchure, or human reed, as it might here be named.

[Sidenote: The French horn.]

[Sidenote: Manipulation of the French horn.]

The French horn (Plate IX.), as it is called in the orchestra, is the sweetest and mellowest of all the wind instruments. In Beethoven's time it was but little else than the old hunting-horn, which, for the convenience of the mounted hunter, was arranged in spiral convolutions that it might be slipped over the head and carried resting on one shoulder and under the opposite arm. The Germans still call it the Waldhorn, i.e., "forest horn;" the old French name was cor de chasse, the Italian corno di caccia. In this instrument formerly the tones which were not the natural resonances of the harmonic division of the tube were helped out by partly closing the bell with the right hand, it having been discovered accidentally that by putting the hand into the lower end of the tube--the flaring part called the bell--the pitch of a tone was raised. Players still make use of this method for convenience, and sometimes because a composer wishes to employ the slightly muffled effect of these tones; but since valves have been added to the instrument, it is possible to play a chromatic scale in what are called the unstopped or open tones.

[Sidenote: Kinds of horns.]

[Sidenote: The trumpet.]

[Sidenote: The cornet.]

Formerly it was necessary to use horns of different pitch, and composers still respect this tradition, and designate the key of the horns which they wish to have employed; but so skilful have the players become that, as a rule, they use horns whose fundamental tone is F for all keys, and achieve the old purpose by simply transposing the music as they read it. If these most graceful instruments were straightened out they would be seventeen feet long. The convolutions of the horn and the many turns of the trumpet are all the fruit of necessity; they could not be manipulated to produce the tones that are asked of them if they were not bent and curved. The trumpet, when its tube is lengthened by the addition of crooks for its lowest key, is eight feet long; the tuba, sixteen. In most orchestras (in all of those in the United States, in fact, except the Boston and Chicago Orchestras and the Symphony Society of New York) the word trumpet is merely a euphemism for cornet, the familiar leading instrument of the brass band, which, while it falls short of the trumpet in the quality of its tone, in the upper registers especially, is a more easily manipulated instrument than the trumpet, and is preferable in the lower tones.

[Sidenote: The trombone.]

Mendelssohn is quoted as saying that the trombones (Plate X.) "are too sacred to use often." They have, indeed, a majesty and nobility all their own, and the lowest use to which they can be put is to furnish a flaring and noisy harmony in an orchestral tutti. They are marvellously expressive instruments, and without a peer in the whole instrumental company when a solemn and spiritually uplifting effect is to be attained. They can also be made to sound menacing and lugubrious, devout and mocking, pompously heroic, majestic, and lofty. They are often the heralds of the orchestra, and make sonorous proclamations.

[Sidenote: Trombone effects.]

[Sidenote: The tuba.]

The classic composers always seemed to approach the trombones with marked respect, but nowadays it requires a very big blue pencil in the hands of a very uncompromising conservatory professor to prevent a student engaged on his Opus 1 from keeping his trombones going half the time at least. It is an old story how Mozart keeps the instruments silent through three-fourths of his immortal "Don Giovanni," so that they may enter with overwhelming impressiveness along with the ghostly visitor of the concluding scene. As a rule, there are three trombones in the modern orchestra--two tenors and a bass. Formerly there were four kinds, bearing the names of the voices to which they were supposed to be nearest in tone-quality and compass--soprano, alto, tenor, and bass. Full four-part harmony is now performed by the three trombones and the tuba (Plate XI.). The latter instrument, which, despite its gigantic size, is exceedingly tractable can "roar you as gently as any sucking dove." Far-away and strangely mysterious tones are got out of the brass instruments, chiefly the cornet and horn, by almost wholly closing the bell.

[Sidenote: Instruments of percussion.]

[Sidenote: The xylophone.]

[Sidenote: Kettle-drums.]

[Sidenote: Pfund's tuning device.]

[Sidenote: Pitch of the drums.]

[Sidenote: Qualifications of a drummer.]

The percussion apparatus of the modern orchestra includes a multitude of instruments scarcely deserving of description. Several varieties of drums, cymbals, triangle, tambourine, steel bars (Glockenspiel), gongs, bells, and many other things which we are now inclined to look upon as toys, rather than as musical instruments, are brought into play for reasons more or less fantastic. Saint-Sa 雗 s has even utilized the barbarous xylophone, whose proper place is the variety hall, in his "Danse Macabre." There his purpose was a fantastic one, and the effect is capital. The pictorial conceit at the bottom of the poem which the music illustrates is Death, as a skeleton, seated on a tombstone, playing the viol, and gleefully cracking his bony heels against the marble. To produce this effect, the composer uses the xylophone with capital results. But of all the ordinary instruments of percussion, the only one that is really musical and deserving of comment is the kettle-drum. This instrument is more musical than the others because it has pitch. Its voice is not mere noise, but musical noise. Kettle-drums, or tympani, are generally used in pairs, though the vast multiplication of effects by modern composers has resulted also in the extension of this department of the band. It is seldom that more than two pairs are used, a good player with a quick ear being able to accomplish all that Wagner asks of six drums by his deftness in changing the pitch of the instruments. This work of tuning is still performed generally in what seems a rudimentary way, though a German drum-builder named Pfund invented a contrivance by which the player, by simply pressing on a balanced pedal and watching an indicator affixed to the side of the drums, can change the pitch to any desired semitone within the range of an octave.

The tympani are hemispherical brass or copper vessels, kettles in short, covered with vellum heads. The pitch of the instrument depends on the tension of the head, which is applied generally by key-screws working through the iron ring which holds the vellum. There is a difference in the size of the drums to place at the command of the player the octave from F in the first space below the bass staff to F on the fourth line of the same staff. Formerly the purpose of the drums was simply to give emphasis, and they were then uniformly tuned to the key-note and fifth of the key in which a composition was set. Now they are tuned in many ways, not only to allow for the frequent change of keys, but also so that they may be used as harmony instruments. Berlioz did more to develop the drums than any composer who has ever lived, though Beethoven already manifested appreciation of their independent musical value. In the last movement of his Eighth Symphony and the scherzo of his Ninth, he tunes them in octaves, his purpose in the latter case being to give the opening figure, an octave leap, of the scherzo melody to the drums solo. The most extravagant use ever made of the drums, however, was by Berlioz in his "Messe des Morts," where he called in eight pairs of drums and ten players to help him to paint his tonal picture of the terrors of the last judgment. The post of drummer is one of the most difficult to fill in a symphonic orchestra. He is required to have not only a perfect sense of time and rhythm, but also a keen sense of pitch, for often the composer asks him to change the pitch of one or both of his drums in the space of a very few seconds. He must then be able to shut all other sounds out of his mind, and bring his drums into a new key while the orchestra is playing--an extremely nice task.

[Sidenote: The bass drum.]

The development of modern orchestral music has given dignity also to the bass drum, which, though definite pitch is denied to it, is now manipulated in a variety of ways productive of striking effects. Rolls are played on it with the sticks of the kettle-drums, and it has been emancipated measurably from the cymbals, which in vulgar brass-band music are its inseparable companions.

[Sidenote: The conductor.]

[Sidenote: Time-beaters and interpreters.]

[Sidenote: The conductor a necessity.]

In the full sense of the term the orchestral conductor is a product of the latter half of the present century. Of course, ever since concerted music began, there has been a musical leader of some kind. Mural paintings and carvings fashioned in Egypt long before Apollo sang his magic song and

"Ilion, like a mist, rose into towers,"

show the conductor standing before his band beating time by clapping his hands; and if we are to credit what we have been told about Hebrew music, Asaph, Heman, and Jeduthun, when they stood before their multitudinous choirs in the temple at Jerusalem, promoted synchronism in the performance by stamping upon the floor with lead-shodden feet. Before the era which developed what I might call "star" conductors, these leaders were but captains of tens and captains of hundreds who accomplished all that was expected of them if they made the performers keep musical step together. They were time-beaters merely--human metronomes. The modern conductor is, in a sense not dreamed of a century ago, a mediator between the composer and the audience. He is a virtuoso who plays upon men instead of a key-board, upon a hundred instruments instead of one. Music differs from her sister arts in many respects, but in none more than in her dependence on the intermediary who stands between her and the people for whose sake she exists. It is this intermediary who wakens her into life.

"Heard melodies are sweet, but those unheard Are sweeter,"

is a pretty bit of hyperbole which involves a contradiction in terms. An unheard melody is no melody at all, and as soon as we have music in which a number of singers or instrumentalists are employed, the taste, feeling, and judgment of an individual are essential to its intelligent and effective publication. In the gentle days of the long ago, when suavity and loveliness of utterance and a recognition of formal symmetry were the "be-all and end-all" of the art, a time-beater sufficed to this end; but now the contents of music are greater, the vessel has been wondrously widened, the language is become curiously complex and ingenious, and no composer of to-day can write down universally intelligible signs for all that he wishes to say. Someone must grasp the whole, expound it to the individual factors which make up the performing sum and provide what is called an interpretation to the public.

[Sidenote: "Star" conductors.]

That someone, of course, is the conductor, and considering the progress that music is continually making it is not at all to be wondered at that he has become a person of stupendous power in the culture of to-day. The one singularity is that he should be so rare. This rarity has had its natural consequence, and the conductor who can conduct, in contradistinction to the conductor who can only beat time, is now a "star." At present we see him going from place to place in Europe giving concerts in which he figures as the principal attraction. The critics discuss his "readings" just as they do the performances of great pianists and singers. A hundred blowers of brass, scrapers of strings, and tootlers on windy wood, labor beneath him transmuting the composer's mysterious symbols into living sound, and when it is all over we frequently find that it seems all to have been done for the greater glory of the conductor instead of the glory of art. That, however, is a digression which it is not necessary to pursue.

[Sidenote: Mistaken popular notions.]

[Sidenote: What the conductor does.]

[Sidenote: Rests and cues.]

Questions and remarks have frequently been addressed to me indicative of the fact that there is a widespread popular conviction that the mission of a conductor is chiefly ornamental at an orchestral concert. That is a sad misconception, and grows out of the old notion that a conductor is only a time-beater. Assuming that the men of the band have played sufficiently together, it is thought that eventually they might keep time without the help of the conductor. It is true that the greater part of the conductor's work is done at rehearsal, at which he enforces upon his men his wishes concerning the speed of the music, expression, and the balance of tone between the different instruments. But all the injunctions given at rehearsal by word of mouth are reiterated by means of a system of signs and signals during the concert performance. Time and rhythm are indicated by the movements of the baton, the former by the speed of the beats, the latter by the direction, the tones upon which the principal stress is to fall being indicated by the down-beat of the baton. The amplitude of the movements also serves to indicate the conductor's wishes concerning dynamic variations, while the left hand is ordinarily used in pantomimic gestures to control individual players or groups. Glances and a play of facial expression also assist in the guidance of the instrumental body. Every musician is expected to count the rests which occur in his part, but when they are of long duration (and sometimes they amount to a hundred measures or more) it is customary for the conductor to indicate the entrance of an instrument by a glance at the player. From this mere outline of the communications which pass between the conductor and his band it will be seen how indispensable he is if music is to have a consistent and vital interpretation.

[Sidenote: Personal magnetism.]

The layman will perhaps also be enabled, by observing the actions of a conductor with a little understanding of their purposes, to appreciate what critics mean when they speak of the "magnetism" of a leader. He will understand that among other things it means the aptitude or capacity for creating a sympathetic relationship between himself and his men which enables him the better by various devices, some arbitrary, some technical and conventional, to imbue them with his thoughts and feelings relative to a composition, and through them to body them forth to the audience.

[Sidenote: The score.]

[Sidenote: Its arrangement.]

[Sidenote: Score reading.]

What it is that the conductor has to guide him while giving his mute commands to his forces may be seen in the reproduction, in the Appendix, of a page from an orchestral score (Plate XII). A score, it will be observed, is a reproduction of all the parts of a composition as they lie upon the desks of the players. The ordering of these parts in the score has not always been as now, but the plan which has the widest and longest approval is that illustrated in our example. The wood-winds are grouped together on the uppermost six staves, the brass in the middle with the tympani separating the horns and trumpets from the trombones, the strings on the lowermost five staves. The example has been chosen because it shows all the instruments of the band employed at once (it is the famous opening tutti of the triumphal march of Beethoven's Fifth Symphony), and is easy of comprehension by musical amateurs for the reason that none of the parts requires transposition except it be an octave up in the case of the piccolo, an instrument of four-foot tone, and an octave down in the case of the double-basses, which are of sixteen-foot tone. All the other parts are to be read as printed, proper attention being given to the alto and tenor clefs used in the parts of the trombones and violas. The ability to "read score" is one of the most essential attributes of a conductor, who, if he have the proper training, can bring all the parts together and reproduce them on the pianoforte, transposing those which do not sound as written and reading the different clefs at sight as he goes along.

V

At an Orchestral Concert

[Sidenote: Classical and Popular.]

[Sidenote: Orchestras and military bands.]

In popular phrase all high-class music is "classical," and all concerts at which such music is played are "classical concerts." Here the word is conceived as the antithesis of "popular," which term is used to designate the ordinary music of the street and music-hall. Elsewhere I have discussed the true meaning of the word and shown its relation to "romantic" in the terminology of musical critics and historians. No harm is done by using both "classical" and "popular" in their common significations, so far as they convey a difference in character between concerts. The highest popular conception of a classical concert is one in which a complete orchestra performs symphonies and extended compositions in allied forms, such as overtures, symphonic poems, and concertos. Change the composition of the instrumental body, by omitting the strings and augmenting the reed and brass choirs, and you have a military band which is best employed in the open air, and whose programmes are generally made up of compositions in the simpler and more easily comprehended forms--dances, marches, fantasias on popular airs, arrangements of operatic excerpts and the like. These, then, are popular concerts in the broadest sense, though it is proper enough to apply the term also to concerts given by a symphonic band when the programme is light in character and aims at more careless diversion than should be sought at a "classical" concert. The latter term, again, is commended to use by the fact that as a rule the music performed at such a concert exemplifies the higher forms in the art, classicism in music being defined as that principle which seeks expression in beauty of form, in a symmetrical ordering of parts and logical sequence, "preferring aesthetic beauty, pure and simple, over emotional content," as I have said in Chapter III.

[Sidenote: The Symphony.]

[Sidenote: Mistaken ideas about the form.]

As the highest type of instrumental music, we take the Symphony. Very rarely indeed is a concert given by an organization like the New York and London Philharmonic Societies, or the Boston and Chicago Orchestras, at which the place of honor in the scheme of pieces is not given to a symphony. Such a concert is for that reason also spoken of popularly as a "Symphony concert," and no confusion would necessarily result from the use of the term even if it so chanced that there was no symphony on the programme. What idea the word symphony conveys to the musically illiterate it would be difficult to tell. I have known a professional writer on musical subjects to express the opinion that a symphony was nothing else than four unrelated compositions for orchestra arranged in a certain sequence for the sake of an agreeable contrast of moods and tempos. It is scarcely necessary to say that the writer in question had a very poor opinion of the Symphony as an Art-form, and believed that it had outlived its usefulness and should be relegated to the limbo of Archaic Things. If he, however, trained in musical history and familiar with musical literature, could see only four unrelated pieces of music in a symphony by Beethoven, we need not marvel that hazy notions touching the nature of the form are prevalent among the untaught public, and that people can be met in concert-rooms to whom such words as "Symphony in C minor," and the printed designations of the different portions of the work-- the "movements," as musicians call them--are utterly bewildering.

[Sidenote: History of the term.]

[Sidenote: Changes in meaning.]

[Sidenote: Handel's "Pastoral Symphony."]

The word symphony has itself a singularly variegated history. Like many another term in music it was borrowed by the modern world from the ancient Greek. To those who coined it, however, it had a much narrower meaning than to us who use it, with only a conventional change in transliteration, now. By [Greek: symphonia] the Greeks simply expressed the concept of agreement, or consonance. Applied to music it meant first such intervals as unisons; then the notion was extended to include consonant harmonies, such as the fifth, fourth, and octave. The study of the ancient theoreticians led the musicians of the Middle Ages to apply the word to harmony in general. Then in some inexplicable fashion it came to stand as a generic term for instrumental compositions such as toccatas, sonatas, etc. Its name was given to one of the precursors of the pianoforte, and in Germany in the sixteenth century the word Symphoney came to mean a town band. In the last century and the beginning of this the term was used to designate an instrumental introduction to a composition for voices, such as a song or chorus, as also an instrumental piece introduced in a choral work. The form, that is the extent and structure of the composition, had nothing to do with the designation, as we see from the Italian shepherds' tune which Handel set for strings in "The Messiah;" he called it simply pifa, but his publishers called it a "Pastoral symphony," and as such we still know it. It was about the middle of the eighteenth century that the present signification became crystallized in the word, and since the symphonies of Haydn, in which the form first reached perfection, are still to be heard in our concert-rooms, it may be said that all the masterpieces of symphonic literature are current.

[Sidenote: The allied forms.]

[Sidenote: Sonata form.]

[Sidenote: Symphony, sonata, and concerto.]

I have already hinted at the fact that there is an intimate relationship between the compositions usually heard at a classical concert. Symphonies, symphonic poems, concertos for solo instruments and orchestra, as well as the various forms of chamber music, such as trios, quartets, and quintets for strings, or pianoforte and strings, are but different expressions of the idea which is best summed up in the word sonata. What musicians call the "sonata form" lies at the bottom of them all--even those which seem to consist of a single piece, like the symphonic poem and overture. Provided it follow, not of necessity slavishly, but in its general structure, a certain scheme which was slowly developed by the geniuses who became the law-givers of the art, a composite or cyclical composition (that is, one composed of a number of parts, or movements) is, as the case may be, a symphony, concerto, or sonata. It is a sonata if it be written for a solo instrument like the pianoforte or organ, or for one like the violin or clarinet, with pianoforte accompaniment. If the accompaniment be written for orchestra, it is called a concerto. A sonata written for an orchestra is a symphony. The nature of the interpreting medium naturally determines the exposition of the form, but all the essential attributes can be learned from a study of the symphony, which because of the dignity and eloquence of its apparatus admits of a wider scope than its allies, and must be accepted as the highest type, not merely of the sonata, but of the instrumental art. It will be necessary presently to point out the more important modifications which compositions of this character have undergone in the development of music, but the ends of clearness will be best subserved if the study be conducted on fundamental lines.

[Sidenote: What a symphony is.]

[Sidenote: The bond of unity between the parts.]

The symphony then, as a rule, is a composition for orchestra made up of four parts, or movements, which are not only related to each other by a bond of sympathy established by the keys chosen but also by their emotional contents. Without this higher bond the unity of the work would be merely mechanical, like the unity accomplished by sameness of key in the old-fashioned suite. (See Chapter VI.) The bond of key-relationship, though no longer so obvious as once it was, is yet readily discovered by a musician; the spiritual bond is more elusive, and presents itself for recognition to the imagination and the feelings of the listener. Nevertheless, it is an element in every truly great symphony, and I have already indicated how it may sometimes become patent to the ear alone, so it be intelligently employed, and enjoy the co-operation of memory.

[Sidenote: The first movement.]

[Sidenote: Exposition of subjects.]

[Sidenote: Repetition of the first subdivision.]

It is the first movement of a symphony which embodies the structural scheme called the "sonata form." It has a triple division, and Mr. Edward Dannreuther has aptly defined it as "the triune symmetry of exposition, illustration, and repetition." In the first division the composer introduces the melodies which he has chosen to be the thematic material of the movement, and to fix the character of the entire work; he presents it for identification. The themes are two, and their exposition generally exemplifies the principle of key-relationship, which was the basis of my analysis of a simple folk tune in Chapter II. In the case of the best symphonists the principal and second subjects disclose a contrast, not violent but yet distinct, in mood or character.

If the first is rhythmically energetic and assertive--masculine, let me say--the second will be more sedate, more gentle in utterance--feminine. After the two subjects have been introduced along with some subsidiary phrases and passages which the composer uses to bind them together and modulate from one key into another, the entire division is repeated. That is the rule, but it is now as often "honored in the breach" as in the observance, some conductors not even hesitating to ignore the repeat marks in Beethoven's scores.

[Sidenote: The free fantasia or "working-out" portion.]

[Sidenote: Repetition.]

The second division is now taken up. In it the composer exploits his learning and fancy in developing his thematic material. He is now entirely free to send it through long chains of keys, to vary the harmonies, rhythms, and instrumentation, to take a single pregnant motive and work it out with all the ingenuity he can muster; to force it up "steep-up spouts" of passion and let it whirl in the surge, or plunge it into "steep-down gulfs of liquid fire," and consume its own heart. Technically this part is called the "free fantasia" in English, and the Durchferung--"working out"--in German. I mention the terms because they sometimes occur in criticisms and analyses. It is in this division that the genius of a composer has fullest play, and there is no greater pleasure, no more delightful excitement, for the symphony-lover than to follow the luminous fancy of Beethoven through his free fantasias. The third division is devoted to a repetition, with modifications, of the first division and the addition of a close.

[Sidenote: Introductions.]

[Sidenote: Keys and Titles.]

First movements are quick and energetic, and frequently full of dramatic fire. In them the psychological story is begun which is to be developed in the remaining chapters of the work--its sorrows, hopes, prayers, or communings in the slow movement; its madness or merriment in the scherzo; its outcome, triumphant or tragic, in the finale. Sometimes the first movement is preceded by a slow introduction, intended to prepare the mind of the listener for the proclamation which shall come with the Allegro. The key of the principal subject is set down as the key of the symphony, and unless the composer gives his work a special title for the purpose of providing a hint as to its poetical contents ("Eroica," "Pastoral," "Faust," "In the Forest," "Lenore," "Pathique," etc.), or to characterize its style ("Scotch," "Italian," "Irish," "Welsh," "Scandinavian," "From the New World"), it is known only by its key, or the number of the work (opus) in the composer's list. Therefore we have Mozart's Symphony "in G minor," Beethoven's "in A major," Schumann's "in C," Brahms's "in F," and so on.

[Sidenote: The second movement.]

[Sidenote: Variations.]

The second movement in the symphonic scheme is the slow movement. Musicians frequently call it the Adagio, for convenience, though the tempi of slow movements ranges from extremely slow (Largo) to the border line of fast, as in the case of the Allegretto of the Seventh Symphony of Beethoven. The mood of the slow movement is frequently sombre, and its instrumental coloring dark; but it may also be consolatory, contemplative, restful, religiously uplifting. The writing is preferably in a broadly sustained style, the effect being that of an exalted hymn, and this has led to a predilection for a theme and variations as the mould in which to cast the movement. The slow movements of Beethoven's Fifth and Ninth Symphonies are made up of variations.

[Sidenote: The Scherzo.]

[Sidenote: Genesis of the Scherzo.]

[Sidenote: The Trio.]

The Scherzo is, as the term implies, the playful, jocose movement of a symphony, but in the case of sublime geniuses like Beethoven and Schumann, who blend profound melancholy with wild humor, the playfulness is sometimes of a kind which invites us to thoughtfulness instead of merriment. This is true also of some Russian composers, whose scherzos have the desperate gayety which speaks from the music of a sad people whose merrymaking is not a spontaneous expression of exuberant spirits but a striving after self-forgetfulness. The Scherzo is the successor of the Minuet, whose rhythm and form served the composers down to Beethoven. It was he who substituted the Scherzo, which retains the chief formal characteristics of the courtly old dance in being in triple time and having a second part called the Trio. With the change there came an increase in speed, but it ought to be remembered that the symphonic minuet was quicker than the dance of the same name. A tendency toward exaggeration, which is patent among modern conductors, is threatening to rob the symphonic minuet of the vivacity which gave it its place in the scheme of the symphony. The entrance of the Trio is marked by the introduction of a new idea (a second minuet) which is more sententious than the first part, and sometimes in another key, the commonest change being from minor to major.

[Sidenote: The Finale.]

[Sidenote: Rondo form.]

The final movement, technically the Finale, is another piece of large dimensions in which the psychological drama which plays through the four acts of the symphony is brought to a conclusion. Once the purpose of the Finale was but to bring the symphony to a merry end, but as the expressive capacity of music has been widened, and mere play with aesthetic forms has given place to attempts to convey sentiments and feelings, the purposes of the last movement have been greatly extended and varied. As a rule the form chosen for the Finale is that called the Rondo. Borrowed from an artificial verse-form (the French Rondeau), this species of composition illustrates the peculiarity of that form in the reiteration of a strophe ever and anon after a new theme or episode has been exploited. In modern society verse, which has grown out of an ambition to imitate the ingenious form invented by medieval poets, we have the Triolet, which may be said to be a rondeau in miniature. I choose one of Mr. H.C. Bunner's dainty creations to illustrate the musical refrain characteristic of the rondo form because of its compactness. Here it is:

[Sidenote: A Rondo pattern in poetry.]

"A pitcher of mignonette In a tenement's highest casement: Queer sort of a flower-pot--yet That pitcher of mignonette Is a garden in heaven set, To the little sick child in the basement-- The pitcher of mignonette, In the tenement's highest casement."

[Sidenote: Other forms for the Finale.]

If now the first two lines of this poem, which compose its refrain, be permitted to stand as the principal theme of a musical piece, we have in Mr. Bunner's triolet a rondo in nuce. There is in it a threefold exposition of the theme alternating with episodic matter. Another form for the finale is that of the first movement (the Sonata form), and still another, the theme and variations. Beethoven chose the latter for his "Eroica," and the choral close of his Ninth, Dvořák, for his symphony in G major, and Brahms for his in E minor.

[Sidenote: Organic Unities.]

[Sidenote: How enforced.]

[Sidenote: Berlioz's "id fixe."]

[Sidenote: Recapitulation of themes.]

I am attempting nothing more than a characterization of the symphony, and the forms with which I associated it at the outset, which shall help the untrained listener to comprehend them as unities despite the fact that to the careless hearer they present themselves as groups of pieces each one of which is complete in itself and has no connection with its fellows. The desire of composers to have their symphonies accepted as unities instead of compages of unrelated pieces has led to the adoption of various devices designed to force the bond of union upon the attention of the hearer. Thus Beethoven in his symphony in C minor not only connects the third and fourth movements but also introduces a reminiscence of the former into the midst of the latter; Berlioz in his "Symphonie Fantastique," which is written to what may be called a dramatic scheme, makes use of a melody which he calls "l'id fixe," and has it recur in each of the four movements as an episode. This, however, is frankly a symphony with programme, and ought not to be treated as a modification of the pure form. Dvorak in his symphony entitled "From the New World," in which he has striven to give expression to the American spirit, quotes the first period of his principal subject in all the subsequent movements, and then sententiously recapitulates the principal themes of the first, second, and third movements in the finale; and this without a sign of the dramatic purpose confessed by Berlioz.

[Sidenote: Introduction of voices.]

[Sidenote: Abolition of pauses.]

In the last movement of his Ninth Symphony Beethoven calls voices to the aid of his instruments. It was a daring innovation, as it seemed to disrupt the form, and we know from the story of the work how long he hunted for the connecting link, which finally he found in the instrumental recitative. Having hit upon the device, he summons each of the preceding movements, which are purely instrumental, into the presence of his augmented forces and dismisses it as inadequate to the proclamation which the symphony was to make. The double-basses and solo barytone are the spokesmen for the tuneful host. He thus achieves the end of connecting the Allegro, Scherzo, and Adagio with each other, and all with the Finale, and at the same time points out what it is that he wishes us to recognize as the inspiration of the whole; but here, again, the means appear to be somewhat extraneous. Schumann's example, however, in abolishing the pauses between the movements of the symphony in D minor, and having melodic material common to all the movements, is a plea for appreciation which cannot be misunderstood. Before Schumann Mendelssohn intended that his "Scotch" symphony should be performed without pauses between the movements, but his wishes have been ignored by the conductors, I fancy because he having neglected to knit the movements together by community of ideas, they can see no valid reason for the abolition of the conventional resting-places.

[Sidenote: Beethoven's "choral" symphony followed.]

Beethoven's augmentation of the symphonic forces by employing voices has been followed by Berlioz in his "Romeo and Juliet," which, though called a "dramatic symphony," is a mixture of symphony, cantata, and opera; Mendelssohn in his "Hymn of Praise" (which is also a composite work and has a composite title--"Symphony Cantata"), and Liszt in his "Faust" symphony, in the finale of which we meet a solo tenor and chorus of men's voices who sing

Goethe's Chorus mysticus.

[Sidenote: Increase in the number of movements.]

A number of other experiments have been made, the effectiveness of which has been conceded in individual instances, but which have failed permanently to affect the symphonic form. Schumann has two trios in his symphony in B-flat, and his E-flat, the so-called "Rhenish," has five movements instead of four, there being two slow movements, one in moderate tempo (Nicht schnell), and the other in slow (Feierlich). In this symphony, also, Schumann exercises the license which has been recognized since Beethoven's time, of changing the places in the scheme of the second and third movements, giving the second place to the jocose division instead of the slow. Beethoven's "Pastoral" has also five movements, unless one chooses to take the storm which interrupts the "Merry-making of the Country Folk" as standing toward the last movement as an introduction, as, indeed, it does in the composer's idyllic scheme. Certain it is, Sir George Grove to the contrary notwithstanding, that the sense of a disturbance of the symphonic plan is not so vivid at a performance of the "Pastoral" as at one of Schumann's "Rhenish," in which either the third movement or the so-called "Cathedral Scene" is most distinctly an interloper.

[Sidenote: Further extension of boundaries.]

[Sidenote: Saint-Sas's C minor symphony.]

Usually it is deference to the demands of a "programme" that influences composers in extending the formal boundaries of a symphony, and when this is done the result is frequently a work which can only be called a symphony by courtesy. M. Saint-Sas, however, attempted an original excursion in his symphony in C minor, without any discoverable, or at least confessed, programmatic idea. He laid the work out in two grand divisions, so as to have but one pause. Nevertheless in each division we can recognize, though as through a haze, the outlines of the familiar symphonic movements. In the first part, buried under a sequence of time designations like this: Adagio--Allegro moderato--Poco adagio, we discover the customary first and second movements, the former preceded by a slow introduction; in the second division we find this arrangement: Allegro moderato--Presto--Maestoso--

Allegro, this multiplicity of terms affording only a sort of disguise for the regulation scherzo and finale, with a cropping out of reminiscences from the first part which have the obvious purpose to impress upon the hearer that the symphony is an organic whole. M. Saint-Sas has also introduced the organ and a pianoforte with two players into the instrumental apparatus.

[Sidenote: The Symphonic Poem.]

[Sidenote: Its characteristics.]

Three characteristics may be said to distinguish the Symphonic Poem, which in the view of the extremists who follow the lead of Liszt is the logical outcome of the symphony and the only expression of its aesthetic principles consonant with modern thought and feeling. First, it is programmatic--that is, it is based upon a poetical idea, a sequence of incidents, or of soul-states, to which a clew is given either by the title or a motto; second, it is compacted in form to a single movement, though as a rule the changing phases delineated in the separate movements of the symphony are also to be found in the divisions of the work marked by changes in tempo, key, and character; third, the work generally has a principal subject of such plasticity that the composer can body forth a varied content by presenting it in a number of transformations.

[Sidenote: Liszt's first pianoforte concerto.]

The last two characteristics Liszt has carried over into his pianoforte concerto in E-flat. This has four distinct movements (viz.: I. Allegro maestoso; II. Quasi adagio; III. _Allegretto vivace, scherzando; IV. Allegro marziale animato_), but they are fused into a continuous whole, throughout which the principal thought of the work, the stupendously energetic phrase which the orchestra proclaims at the outset, is presented in various forms to make it express a great variety of moods and yet give unity to the concerto. "Thus, by means of this metamorphosis," says Mr. Edward Dannreuther, "the poetic unity of the whole musical tissue is made apparent, spite of very great diversity of details; and Coleridge's attempt at a definition of poetic unity--unity in multiety--is carried out to the letter."

[Sidenote: Other cyclical forms.]

[Sidenote: Pianoforte and orchestra.]

It will readily be understood that the other cyclical compositions which I have associated with a classic concert, that is, compositions belonging to the category of chamber music (see Chapter III.), and concertos for solo instruments with orchestral accompaniment, while conforming to the scheme which I have outlined, all have individual characteristics conditioned on the expressive capacity of the apparatus. The modern pianoforte is capable of asserting itself against a full orchestra, and concertos have been written for it in which it is treated as an orchestral integer rather than a solo instrument. In the older conception, the orchestra, though it frequently assumed the privilege of introducing the subject-matter, played a subordinate part to the solo instrument in its development. In violin as well as pianoforte concertos special opportunity is given to the player to exploit his skill and display the solo instrument free from structural restrictions in the cadenza introduced shortly before the close of the first, last, or both movements.

[Sidenote: Cadenzas.]

[Sidenote: Improvisations by the player.]

[Sidenote: M. Ysaye's opinion of Cadenzas.]

Cadenzas are a relic of a time when the art of improvisation was more generally practised than it is now, and when performers were conceded to have rights beyond the printed page. Solely for their display, it became customary for composers to indicate by a hold ([fermata symbol]) a place where the performer might indulge in a flourish of his own. There is a tradition that Mozart once remarked: "Wherever I smear that thing," indicating a hold, "you can do what you please;" the rule is, however, that the only privilege which the cadenza opens to the player is that of improvising on material drawn from the subjects already developed, and since, also as a rule, composers are generally more eloquent in the treatment of their own ideas than performers, it is seldom that a cadenza contributes to the enjoyment afforded by a work, except to the lovers of technique for technique's sake. I never knew an artist to make a more sensible remark than did M. Ysaye, when on the eve of a memorably beautiful performance of Beethoven's violin concerto, he said: "If I were permitted to consult my own wishes I would put my violin under my arm when I reach the fermate and say: 'Ladies and gentlemen, we have reached the cadenza. It is presumptuous in any musician to think that he can have anything to say after Beethoven has finished. With your permission we will consider my cadenza played.'" That Beethoven may himself have had a thought of the same nature is a fair inference from the circumstance that he refused to leave the cadenza in his E-flat pianoforte concerto to the mercy of the virtuosos but wrote it himself.

[Sidenote: Concertos.]

[Sidenote: Chamber music.]

Concertos for pianoforte or violin are usually written in three movements, of which the first and last follow the symphonic model in respect of elaboration and form, and the second is a brief movement in slow or moderate time, which has the character of an intermezzo. As to the nomenclature of chamber music, it is to be noted that unless connected with a qualifying word or phrase, "Quartet" means a string quartet. When a pianoforte is consorted with strings the work is spoken of as a Pianoforte Trio, Quartet, or Quintet, as the case may be.

[Sidenote: The Overture.]

[Sidenote: Pot-pourris.]

The form of the overture is that of the first movement of the sonata, or symphony, omitting the repetition of the first subdivision. Since the original purpose, which gave the overture its name (Ouverture = aperture, opening), was to introduce a drama, either spoken or lyrical, an oratorio, or other choral composition, it became customary for the composers to choose the subjects of the piece from the climacteric moments of the music used in the drama. When done without regard to the rules of construction (as is the case with practically all operetta overtures and Rossini's) the result is not an overture at all, but a pot-pourri, a hotch-potch of jingles. The present beautiful form, in which Beethoven and other composers have shown that it is possible to epitomize an entire drama, took the place of an arbitrary scheme which was wholly aimless, so far as the compositions to which they were attached were concerned.

[Sidenote: Old styles of overtures.]

[Sidenote: The Prelude.]

[Sidenote: Gluck's principle.]

[Sidenote: Descriptive titles.]

The earliest fixed form of the overture is preserved to the current lists of to-day by the compositions of Bach and Handel. It is that established by Lully, and is tripartite in form, consisting of a rapid movement, generally a fugue, preceded and followed by a slow movement which is grave and stately in its tread. In its latest phase the overture has yielded up its name in favor of Prelude (German, Vorspiel), Introduction, or Symphonic Prologue. The finest of these, without borrowing their themes from the works which they introduce, but using new matter entirely, seek to fulfil the aim which Gluck set for himself, when, in the preface to "Alceste," he wrote: "I imagined that the overture ought to prepare the audience for the action of the piece, and serve as a kind of argument to it." Concert overtures are compositions designed by the composers to stand as independent pieces instead of for performance in connection with a drama, opera, or oratorio. When, as is frequently the case, the composer, nevertheless, gives them a descriptive title ("Hebrides," "Sakuntala"), their poetical contents are to be sought in the associations aroused by the title. Thus, in the instances cited, "Hebrides" suggests that the overture was designed by Mendelssohn to reflect the mood awakened in him by a visit to the Hebrides, more particularly to Fingal's Cave (wherefore the overture is called the "Fingal's Cave" overture in Germany)--"Sakuntala" invites to a study of Kalidasa's drama of that name as the repository of the sentiments which Goldmark undertook to express in his music.

[Sidenote: Serenades.]

[Sidenote: The Serenade in Shakespeare.]

A form which is variously employed, for solo instruments, small combinations, and full orchestra (though seldom with the complete modern apparatus), is the Serenade. Historically, it is a contemporary of the old suites and the first symphonies, and like them it consists of a group of short pieces, so arranged as to form an agreeable contrast with each other, and yet convey a sense of organic unity. The character of the various parts and their order grew out of the purpose for which the serenade was originated, which was that indicated by the name. In the last century, and earlier, it was no uncommon thing for a lover to bring the tribute of a musical performance to his mistress, and it was not always a "woful ballad" sung to her eyebrow. Frequently musicians were hired, and the tribute took the form of a nocturnal concert. In Shakespeare's "Two Gentlemen of Verona," Proteus, prompting Thurio what to do to win Silvia's love, says:

"Visit by night your lady's chamber window With some sweet concert: to their instruments Tune a deploring dump; the night's dread silence Will well become such sweet complaining grievance."

[Sidenote: Out-of-doors music.]

[Sidenote: Old forms.]

[Sidenote: The "Dump."]

[Sidenote: Beethoven's Serenade, op. 8.]

It was for such purposes that the serenade was invented as an instrumental form. Since they were to play out of doors, _Sir Thurio's_ musicians would have used wind instruments instead of viols, and the oldest serenades are composed for oboes and bassoons. Clarinets and horns were subsequently added, and for such bands Mozart wrote serenades, some of which so closely approach the symphony that they have been published as symphonies. A serenade in the olden time opened very properly with a march, to the strains of which we may imagine the musicians approaching the lady's chamber window. Then came a minuet to prepare her ear for the "deploring dump" which followed, the "dump" of Shakespeare's day, like the "dumka" of ours (with which I am tempted to associate it etymologically), being a mournful piece of music most happily characterized by the poet as a "sweet complaining grievance." Then followed another piece in merry tempo and rhythm, then a second adagio, and the entertainment ended with an allegro, generally in march rhythm, to which we fancy the musicians departing. The order is exemplified in Beethoven's serenade for violin, viola, and violoncello, op. 8, which runs thus: March; Adagio; Minuet; Adagio with episodic Scherzo; Polacca; Andante (variations), the opening march repeated.

[Sidenote: The Orchestral Suite.]

[Sidenote: Ballet music.]

The Suite has come back into favor as an orchestral piece, but the term no longer has the fixed significance which once it had. It is now applied to almost any group of short pieces, pleasantly contrasted in rhythm, tempo, and mood, each complete in itself yet disclosing an aesthetic relationship with its fellows. Sometimes old dance forms are used, and sometimes new, such as the polonaise and the waltz. The ballet music, which fills so welcome a place in popular programmes, may be looked upon as such a suite, and the rhythm of the music and the orchestral coloring in them are frequently those peculiar to the dances of the countries in which the story of the opera or drama for which the music was written plays. The ballets therefore afford an excellent opportunity for the study of local color. Thus the ballet music from Massenet's "Cid" is Spanish, from Rubinstein's "Feramors" Oriental, from "Aida" Egyptian--Oriental rhythms and colorings being those most easily copied by composers.

[Sidenote: Operatic excerpts.]

[Sidenote: Gluck and Vestris.]

The other operatic excerpts common to concerts of both classes are either between-acts music, fantasias on operatic airs, or, in the case of Wagner's contributions, portions of his dramas which are so predominantly instrumental that it has been found feasible to incorporate the vocal part with the orchestral. In ballet music from the operas of the last century, some of which has been preserved to the modern concert-room, local color must not be sought. Gluck's Greeks, like Shakespeare's, danced to the rhythms of the seventeenth century. Vestris, whom the people of his time called "The god of the dance," once complained to Gluck that his "Iphig 閗 ie en Aulide" did not end with a chaconne, as was the rule. "A chaconne!" cried Gluck; "when did the Greeks ever dance a chaconne?" "Didn't they? Didn't they?" answered Vestris; "so much the worse for the Greeks." There ensued a quarrel. Gluck became incensed, withdrew the opera which was about to be produced, and would have left Paris had not Marie Antoinette come to the rescue. But Vestris got his chaconne.

VI

At a Pianoforte Recital

[Sidenote: Mr. Paderewski's concerts.]

No clearer illustration of the magical power which lies in music, no more convincing proof of the puissant fascination which a musical artist can exert, no greater demonstration of the capabilities of an instrument of music can be imagined than was afforded by the pianoforte recitals which Mr. Paderewski gave in the United States during the season of 1895-96. More than threescore times in the course of five months, in the principal cities of this country, did this wonderful man seat himself in the presence of audiences, whose numbers ran into the thousands, and were limited only by the seating capacity of the rooms in which they gathered, and hold them spellbound from two to three hours by the eloquence of his playing. Each time the people came in a gladsome frame of mind, stimulated by the recollection of previous delights or eager expectation. Each time they sat listening to the music as if it were an evangel on which hung everlasting things. Each time there was the same growth in enthusiasm which began in decorous applause and ended in cheers and shouts as the artist came back after the performance of a herculean task, and added piece after piece to a programme which had been laid down on generous lines from the beginning. The careless saw the spectacle with simple amazement, but for the judicious it had a wondrous interest.

[Sidenote: Pianoforte recitals.]

[Sidenote: The pianoforte's underlying principles.]

I am not now concerned with Mr. Paderewski beyond invoking his aid in bringing into court a form of entertainment which, in his hands, has proved to be more attractive to the multitude than symphony, oratorio, and even opera. What a world of speculation and curious inquiry does such a recital invite one into, beginning with the instrument which was the medium of communication between the artist and his hearers! To follow the progressive development of the mechanical principles underlying the pianoforte, one would be obliged to begin beyond the veil which separates history from tradition, for the first of them finds its earliest exemplification in the bow twanged by the primitive savage. Since a recognition of these principles may help to an understanding of the art of pianoforte playing, I enumerate them now. They are:

1. A stretched string as a medium of tone production.

2. A key-board as an agency for manipulating the strings.

3. A blow as the means of exciting the strings to vibratory action, by which the tone is produced.

[Sidenote: Their Genesis.]

[Sidenote: Significance of the pianoforte.]

Many interesting glimpses of the human mind and heart might we have in the course of the promenade through the ancient, medieval, and modern worlds which would be necessary to disclose the origin and growth of these three principles, but these we must forego, since we are to study the music of the instrument, not its history. Let the knowledge suffice that the fundamental principle of the pianoforte is as old as music itself, and that scientific learning, inventive ingenuity, and mechanical skill, tributary always to the genius of the art, have worked together for centuries to apply this principle, until the instrument which embodies it in its highest potency is become a veritable microcosm of music. It is the visible sign of culture in every gentle household; the indispensable companion of the composer and teacher; the intermediary between all the various branches of music. Into the study of the orchestral conductor it brings a translation of all the multitudinous voices of the band; to the choir-master it represents the chorus of singers in the church-loft or on the concert-platform; with its aid the opera director fills his imagination with the people, passions, and pageantry of the lyric drama long before the singers have received their parts, or the costumer, stage manager, and scene-painter have begun their work. It is the only medium through which the musician in his study can commune with the whole world of music and all its heroes; and though it may fail to inspire somewhat of that sympathetic nearness which one feels toward the violin as it nestles under the chin and throbs synchronously with the player's emotions, or those wind instruments into which the player breathes his own breath as the breath of life, it surpasses all its rivals, save the organ, in its capacity for publishing the grand harmonies of the masters, for uttering their "sevenfold chorus of hallelujahs and harping symphonies."

[Sidenote: Defects of the pianoforte.]

[Sidenote: Lack of sustaining power.]

This is one side of the picture and serves to show why the pianoforte is the most universal, useful, and necessary of all musical instruments. The other side shows its deficiencies, which must also be known if one is to appreciate rightly the many things he is called upon to note while listening intelligently to pianoforte music. Despite all the skill, learning, and ingenuity which have been spent on its perfection, the pianoforte can be made only feebly to approximate that sustained style of musical utterance which is the soul of melody, and finds its loftiest exemplification in singing. To give out a melody perfectly, presupposes the capacity to sustain tones without loss in power or quality, to bind them together at will, and sometimes to intensify their dynamic or expressive force while they sound. The tone of the pianoforte, being produced by a blow, begins to die the moment it is created. The history of the instrument's mechanism, and also of its technical manipulation, is the history of an effort to reduce this shortcoming to a minimum. It has always conditioned the character of the music composed for the instrument, and if we were not in danger of being led into too wide an excursion, it would be profitable to trace the parallelism which is disclosed by the mechanical evolution of the instrument, and the technical and spiritual evolution of the music composed for it. A few points will be touched upon presently, when the intellectual activity invited by a recital is brought under consideration.

[Sidenote: The percussive element.]

[Sidenote: Melody with drum-beats.]

[Sidenote: Rhythmical accentuation.]

[Sidenote: A universal substitute.]

It is to be noted, further, that by a beautiful application of the doctrine of compensations, the factor which limits the capacity of the pianoforte as a melody instrument endows it with a merit which no other instrument has in the same degree, except the instruments of percussion, which, despite their usefulness, stand on the border line between savage and civilized music. It is from its relationship to the drum that the pianoforte derives a peculiarity quite unique in the melodic and harmonic family. Rhythm is, after all, the starting-point of music. More than melody, more than harmony, it stirs the blood of the savage, and since the most vital forces within man are those which date back to his primitive state, so the sense of rhythm is the most universal of the musical senses among even the most cultured of peoples to-day. By themselves the drums, triangles, and cymbals of an orchestra represent music but one remove from noise; but everybody knows how marvellously they can be utilized to glorify a climax. Now, in a very refined degree, every melody on the pianoforte, be it played as delicately as it may, is a melody with drum-beats. Manufacturers have done much toward eliminating the thump of the hammers against the strings, and familiarity with the tone of the instrument has closed our ears against it to a great extent as something intrusive, but the blow which excites the string to vibration, and thus generates sound, is yet a vital factor in determining the character of pianoforte music. The recurrent pulsations, now energetic, incisive, resolute, now gentle and caressing, infuse life into the melody, and by emphasizing its rhythmical structure (without unduly exaggerating it), present the form of the melody in much sharper outline than is possible on any other instrument, and much more than one would expect in view of the evanescent character of the pianoforte's tone. It is this quality, combined with the mechanism which places all the gradations of tone, from loudest to softest, at the easy and instantaneous command of the player, which, I fancy, makes the pianoforte, in an astonishing degree, a substitute for all the other instruments. Each instrument in the orchestra has an idiom, which sounds incomprehensible when uttered by some other of its fellows, but they can all be translated, with more or less success, into the language of the pianoforte--not the quality of the tone, though even that can be suggested, but the character of the phrase. The pianoforte can sentimentalize like the flute, make a martial proclamation like the trumpet, intone a prayer like the churchly trombone.

[Sidenote: The instrument's mechanism.]

[Sidenote: Tone formation and production.]

In the intricacy of its mechanism the pianoforte stands next to the organ. The farther removed from direct utterance we are the more difficult is it to speak the true language of music. The violin player and the singer, and in a less degree the performers upon some of the wind instruments, are obliged to form the musical tone--which, in the case of the pianist, is latent in the instrument, ready to present itself in two of its attributes in answer to a simple pressure upon the key. The most unmusical person in the world can learn to produce a series of tones from a pianoforte which shall be as exact in pitch and as varied in dynamic force as can Mr. Paderewski. He cannot combine them so ingeniously nor imbue them with feeling, but in the simple matter of producing the tone with the attributes mentioned, he is on a level with the greatest virtuoso. Very different is the case of the musician who must exercise a distinctly musical gift in the simple evocation of the materials of music, like the violinist and singer, who both form and produce the tone. For them compensation flows from the circumstance that the tone thus formed and produced is naturally instinct with emotional life in a degree that the pianoforte tone knows nothing of.

[Sidenote: Technical manipulation.]

[Sidenote: Touch and emotionality.]

In one respect, it may be said that the mechanics of pianoforte playing represent a low plane of artistic activity, a fact which ought always to be remembered whenever the temptation is felt greatly to exalt the technique of the art; but it must also be borne in mind that the mechanical nature of simple tone production in pianoforte playing raises the value of the emotional quality which, nevertheless, stands at the command of the player.

The emotional potency of the tone must come from the manner in which the blow is given to the string. Recognition of this fact has stimulated reflection, and this in turn has discovered methods by which temperament and emotionality may be made to express themselves as freely, convincingly, and spontaneously in pianoforte as in violin playing. If this were not so it would be impossible to explain the difference in the charm exerted by different virtuosi, for it has frequently happened that the best-equipped mechanician and the most intellectual player has been judged inferior as an artist to another whose gifts were of the soul rather than of the brains and fingers.

[Sidenote: The technical cult.]

[Sidenote: A low form of art.]

The feats accomplished by a pianoforte virtuoso in the mechanical department are of so extraordinary a nature that there need be small wonder at the wide prevalence of a distinctly technical cult. All who know the real nature and mission of music must condemn such a cult. It is a sign of a want of true appreciation to admire technique for technique's sake. It is a mistaking of the outward shell for the kernel, a means for the end. There are still many players who aim to secure this admiration, either because they are deficient in real musical feeling, or because they believe themselves surer of winning applause by thus appealing to the lowest form of appreciation. In the early part of the century they would have been handicapped by the instrument which lent itself to delicacy, clearness, and gracefulness of expression, but had little power. Now the pianoforte has become a thing of rigid steel, enduring tons of strain from its strings, and having a voice like the roar of many waters; to keep pace with it players have become athletes with

"Thews of Anakim And pulses of a Titan's heart."

[Sidenote: Technical skill a matter of course.]

They care no more for the "murmurs made to bless," unless it be occasionally for the sake of contrast, but seek to astound, amaze, bewilder, and confound with feats of skill and endurance. That with their devotion to the purely mechanical side of the art they are threatening to destroy pianoforte playing gives them no pause whatever. The era which they illustrate and adorn is the technical era which was, is, and ever shall be, the era of decay in artistic production. For the judicious technique alone, be it never so marvellous, cannot serve to-day. Its possession is accepted as a condition precedent in the case of everyone who ventures to appear upon the concert-platform. He must be a wonder, indeed, who can disturb our critical equilibrium by mere digital feats. We want strength and velocity of finger to be coupled with strength, velocity, and penetration of thought. We want no halting or lisping in the proclamation of what the composer has said, but we want the contents of his thought, not the hollow shell, no matter how distinctly its outlines be drawn.

[Sidenote: The plan of study in this chapter.]

[Sidenote: A typical scheme of pieces.]

The factors which present themselves for consideration at a pianoforte recital--mechanical, intellectual, and emotional--can be most intelligently and profitably studied along with the development of the instrument and its music. All branches of the study are invited by the typical recital programme. The essentially romantic trend of Mr. Paderewski's nature makes his excursions into the classical field few and short; and it is only when a pianist undertakes to emulate Rubinstein in his historical recitals that the entire pre-Beethoven vista is opened up. It will suffice for the purposes of this discussion to imagine a programme containing pieces by Bach, D. Scarlatti, Handel, and Mozart in one group; a sonata by Beethoven; some of the shorter pieces of Schumann and Chopin, and one of the transcriptions or rhapsodies of Liszt.

[Sidenote: Periods in pianoforte music.]

Such a scheme falls naturally into four divisions, plainly differentiated from each other in respect of the style of composition and the manner of performance, both determined by the nature of the instrument employed and the status of the musical idea. Simply for the sake of convenience let the period represented by the first group be called the classic; the second the classic-romantic; the third the romantic, and the last the bravura. I beg the reader, however, not to extend these designations beyond the boundaries of the present study; they have been chosen arbitrarily, and confusion might result if the attempt were made to apply them to any particular concert scheme. I have chosen the composers because of their broadly representative capacity. And they must stand for a numerous epigonoi whose names make up our concert lists: say, Couperin, Rameau, and Haydn in the first group; Schubert in the second; Mendelssohn and Rubinstein in the third. It would not be respectful to the memory of Liszt were I to give him the associates with whom in my opinion he stands; that matter may be held in abeyance.

[Sidenote: Predecessors of the pianoforte.]

[Sidenote: The Clavichord.]

[Sidenote: "Bebung."]

The instruments for which the first group of writers down to Haydn and Mozart wrote, were the immediate precursors of the pianoforte--the clavichord, spinet, or virginal, and harpsichord. The last was the concert instrument, and stood in the same relationship to the others that the grand pianoforte of to-day stands to the upright and square. The clavichord was generally the medium for the composer's private communings with his muse, because of its superiority over its fellows in expressive power; but it gave forth only a tiny tinkle and was incapable of stirring effects beyond those which sprang from pure emotionality. The tone was produced by a blow against the string, delivered by a bit of brass set in the farther end of the key. The action was that of a direct lever, and the bit of brass, which was called the tangent, also acted as a bridge and measured off the segment of string whose vibration produced the desired tone. It was therefore necessary to keep the key pressed down so long as it was desired that the tone should sound, a fact which must be kept in mind if one would understand the shortcomings as well as the advantages of the instrument compared with the spinet or harpsichord. It also furnishes one explanation of the greater lyricism of Bach's music compared with that of his contemporaries. By gently rocking the hand while the key was down, a tremulous motion could be communicated to the string, which not only prolonged the tone appreciably but gave it an expressive effect somewhat analogous to the vibrato of a violinist. The Germans called this effect Bebung, the French Balancement, and it was indicated by a row of dots under a short slur written over the note. It is to the special fondness which Bach felt for the clavichord that we owe, to a great extent, the cantabile style of his music, its many-voicedness and its high emotionality.

[Sidenote: Quilled instruments.]

[Sidenote: Tone of the harpsichord and spinet.]

[Sidenote: Bach's "Music of the future."]

The spinet, virginal, and harpsichord were quilled instruments, the tone of which was produced by snapping the strings by means of plectra made of quill, or some other flexible substance, set in the upper end of a bit of wood called the jack, which rested on the farther end of the key and moved through a slot in the sounding-board. When the key was pressed down, the jack moved upward past the string which was caught and twanged by the plectrum. The blow of the clavichord tangent could be graduated like that of the pianoforte hammer, but the quills of the other instruments always plucked the strings with the same force, so that mechanical devices, such as a swell-box, similar in principle to that of the organ, coupling in octaves, doubling the strings, etc., had to be resorted to for variety of dynamic effects. The character of tone thus produced determined the character of the music composed for these instruments to a great extent. The brevity of the sound made sustained melodies ineffective, and encouraged the use of a great variety of embellishments and the spreading out of harmonies in the form of arpeggios. It is obvious enough that Bach, being one of those monumental geniuses that cast their prescient vision far into the future, refused to be bound by such mechanical limitations. Though he wrote Clavier, he thought organ, which was his true interpretative medium, and so it happens that the greatest sonority and the broadest style that have been developed in the pianoforte do not exhaust the contents of such a composition as the "Chromatic Fantasia and Fugue."

[Sidenote: Scarlatti's sonatas.]

The earliest music written for these instruments--music which does not enter into this study--was but one remove from vocal music. It came through compositions written for the organ. Of Scarlatti's music the pieces most familiar are a Capriccio and Pastorale which Tausig rewrote for the pianoforte.

They were called sonatas by their composer, but are not sonatas in the modern sense. Sonata means "sound-piece," and when the term came into music it signified only that the composition to which it was applied was written for instruments instead of voices. Scarlatti did a great deal to develop the technique of the harpsichord and the style of composing for it. His sonatas consist each of a single movement only, but in their structure they foreshadow the modern sonata form in having two contrasted themes, which are presented in a fixed key-relationship. They are frequently full of grace and animation, but are as purely objective, formal, and soulless in their content as the other instrumental compositions of the epoch to which they belong.

[Sidenote: The suite.]

[Sidenote: Its history and form.]

[Sidenote: The bond between the movements.]

The most significant of the compositions of this period are the Suites, which because they make up so large a percentage of Clavier literature (using the term to cover the pianoforte and its predecessors), and because they pointed the way to the distinguishing form of the subsequent period, the sonata, are deserving of more extended consideration. The suite is a set of pieces in the same key, but contrasted in character, based upon certain admired dance-forms. Originally it was a set of dances and nothing more, but in the hands of the composers the dances underwent many modifications, some of them to the obvious detriment of their national or other distinguishing characteristics. The suite came into fashion about the middle of the seventeenth century and was also called Sonata da Camera and Balletto in Italy, and, later, Partita in France. In its fundamental form it embraced four movements: I. Allemande. II. Courante. III. Sarabande. IV. Gigue. To these four were sometimes added other dances--the Gavotte, Passepied, Branle, Minuet, Bourre, etc.--but the rule was that they should be introduced between the Sarabande and the Gigue. Sometimes also the set was introduced by a Prelude or an Overture. Identity of key was the only external tie between the various members of the suite, but the composers sought to establish an artistic unity by elaborating the sentiments for which the dance-forms seemed to offer a vehicle, and presenting them in agreeable contrast, besides enriching the primitive structure with new material. The suites of Bach and Handel are the high-water mark in this style of composition, but it would be difficult to find the original characteristics of the dances in their settings. It must suffice us briefly to indicate the characteristics of the principal forms.

[Sidenote: The Allemande.]

The Allemande, as its name indicates, was a dance of supposedly German origin. For that reason the German composers, when it came to them from France, where the suite had its origin, treated it with great partiality. It is in moderate tempo, common time, and made up of two periods of eight measures, both of which are repeated. It begins with an upbeat, and its metre, to use the terms of prosody, is iambic. The following specimen from Mersenne's "Harmonie Universelle," 1636, well displays its characteristics:

[Sidenote: Iambics in music and poetry.]

Robert Burns's familiar iambics,

"Ye flowery banks o' bonnie Doon, How can ye bloom sae fair? How can ye chant, ye little birds, And I sae fu' o' care!"

might serve to keep the rhythmical characteristics of the Allemande in mind were it not for the arbitrary changes made by the composers already hinted at. As it is, we frequently find the stately movement of the old dance broken up into elaborate, but always quietly flowing, ornamentation, as indicated in the following excerpt from the third of Bach's English suites:

[Sidenote: The Courante.]

The Courante, or Corrente ("Teach lavoltas high and swift corantos," says Shakespeare), is a French dance which was extremely popular in the sixteenth, seventeenth, and eighteenth centuries--a polite dance, like the minuet. It was in triple time, and its movement was bright and brisk, a merry energy being imparted to the measure by the prevailing figure, a dotted quarter-note, an eighth, and a quarter in a measure, as illustrated in the following excerpt also from Mersenne:

The suite composers varied the movement greatly, however, and the Italian

Corrente consists chiefly of rapid running passages.

[Sidenote: The Sarabande.]

The Sarabande was also in triple time, but its movement was slow and stately. In Spain, whence it was derived, it was sung to the accompaniment of castanets, a fact which in itself suffices to indicate that it was originally of a lively character, and took on its solemnity in the hands of the later composers. Handel found the Sarabande a peculiarly admirable vehicle for his inspirations, and one of the finest examples extant figures in the triumphal music of his "Almira," composed in 1704:

[Sidenote: A Sarabande by Handel.]

Seven years after the production of "Almira," Handel recurred to this beautiful instrumental piece, and out of it constructed the exquisite lament beginning "Lascia ch'io pianga" in his opera "Rinaldo."

[Sidenote: The Gigue.]

[Sidenote: The Minuet.]

[Sidenote: The Gavotte.]

Great Britain's contribution to the Suite was the final Gigue, which is our jolly and familiar friend the jig, and in all probability is Keltic in origin. It is, as everybody knows, a rollicking measure in 6-8, 12-8, or 4-4 time, with twelve triplet quavers in a measure, and needs no description. It remained a favorite with composers until far into the eighteenth century. Shakespeare proclaims its exuberant lustiness when he makes Sir Toby Belch protest that had he _Sir Andrew's_ gifts his "very walk should be a jig." Of the other dances incorporated into the suite, two are deserving of special mention because of their influence on the music of to-day--the Minuet, which is the parent of the symphonic scherzo, and the Gavotte, whose fascinating movement is frequently heard in latter-day operettas. The Minuet is a French dance, and came from Poitou. Louis XIV. danced it to Lully's music for the first time at Versailles in 1653, and it soon became the most popular of court and society dances, holding its own down to the beginning of the nineteenth century. It was long called the Queen of Dances, and there is no one who has grieved to see the departure of gallantry and grace from our ball-rooms but will wish to see Her Gracious Majesty restored to her throne. The music of the minuet is in 3-4 time, and of stately movement. The Gavotte is a lively dance-measure in common time, beginning, as a rule, on the third beat. Its origin has been traced to the mountain people of the Dauphin called Gavots--whence its name.

[Sidenote: Technique of the Clavier players.]

[Sidenote: Change in technique.]

The transferrence of this music to the modern pianoforte has effected a vast change in the manner of its performance. In the period under consideration emotionality, which is considered the loftiest attribute of pianoforte playing to-day, was lacking, except in the case of such masters of the clavichord as the great Bach and his son, Carl Philipp Emanuel, who inherited his father's preference for that instrument over the harpsichord and pianoforte. Tastefulness in the giving out of the melody, distinctness of enunciation, correctness of phrasing, nimbleness and lightness of finger, summed up practically all that there was in virtuosoship. Intellectuality and digital skill were the essential factors. Beauty of tone through which feeling and temperament speak now was the product of the maker of the instrument, except again in the case of the clavichord, in which it may have been largely the creation of the player. It is, therefore, not surprising that the first revolution in technique of which we hear was accomplished by Bach, who, the better to bring out the characteristics of his polyphonic style, made use of the thumb, till then considered almost a useless member of the hand in playing, and bent his fingers, so that their movements might be more unconstrained.

[Sidenote: Bach's touch.]

[Sidenote: Handel's playing.]

[Sidenote: Scarlatti's style.]

Of the varieties of touch, which play such a role in pianoforte pedagogics to-day, nothing was known. Only on the clavichord was a blow delivered directly against the string, and, as has already been said, only on that instrument was the dynamic shading regulated by the touch. Practically, the same touch was used on the organ and the stringed instruments with key-board. When we find written praise of the old players it always goes to the fluency and lightness of their fingering. Handel was greatly esteemed as a harpsichord player, and seems to have invented a position of the hand like Bach's, or to have copied it from that master. Forkel tells us the movement of Bach's fingers was so slight as to be scarcely noticeable; the position of his hands remained unchanged throughout, and the rest of his body motionless. Speaking of Handel's harpsichord playing, Burney says that his fingers "seemed to grow to the keys. They were so curved and compact when he played that no motion, and scarcely the fingers themselves, could be discovered." Scarlatti's significance lies chiefly in an extension of the technique of his time so as to give greater individuality to the instrument. He indulged freely in brilliant passages and figures which sometimes call for a crossing of the hands, also in leaps of over an octave, repetition of a note by different fingers, broken chords in contrary motion, and other devices which prefigure modern pianoforte music.

[Sidenote: The sonata.]

That Scarlatti also pointed the way to the modern sonata, I have already said. The history of the sonata, as the term is now understood, ends with Beethoven. Many sonatas have been written since the last one of that great master, but not a word has been added to his proclamation. He stands, therefore, as a perfect exemplar of the second period in the scheme which we have adopted for the study of pianoforte music and playing. In a general way a sonata may be described as a composition of four movements, contrasted in mood, tempo, sentiment, and character, but connected by that spiritual bond of which mention was made in our study of the symphony. In short, a sonata is a symphony for a solo instrument.

[Sidenote: Haydn.]

When it came into being it was little else than a convenient formula for the expression of musical beauty. Haydn, who perfected it on its formal side, left it that and nothing more. Mozart poured the vessel full of beauty, but

Beethoven breathed the breath of a new life into it. An old writer tells us of Haydn that he was wont to say that the whole art of composing consisted in taking up a subject and pursuing it. Having invented his theme, he would begin by choosing the keys through which he wished to make it pass.

"His exquisite feeling gave him a perfect knowledge of the greater or less degree of effect which one chord produces in succeeding another, and he afterward imagined a little romance which might furnish him with sentiments and colors."

[Sidenote: Beethoven.]

[Sidenote: Mozart's manner of playing.]

Beethoven began with the sentiment and worked from it outwardly, modifying the form when it became necessary to do so, in order to obtain complete and perfect utterance. He made spirit rise superior to matter. This must be borne in mind when comparing the technique of the previous period with that of which I have made Beethoven the representative. In the little that we are privileged to read of Mozart's style of playing, we see only a reflex of the players who went before him, saving as it was permeated by the warmth which went out from his own genial personality. His manipulation of the keys had the quietness and smoothness that were praised in Bach and Handel.

"Delicacy and taste," says Kullak, "with his lifting of the entire technique to the spiritual aspiration of the idea, elevate him as a virtuoso to a height unanimously conceded by the public, by connoisseurs, and by artists capable of judging. Clementi declared that he had never heard any one play so soulfully and charmfully as Mozart; Dittersdorf finds art and taste combined in his playing; Haydn asseverated with tears that Mozart's playing he could never forget, for it touched the heart. His staccato is said to have possessed a peculiarly brilliant charm."

[Sidenote: Clementi.]

[Sidenote: Beethoven as a pianist.]

The period of C.P.E. Bach, Haydn, and Mozart is that in which the pianoforte gradually replaced its predecessors, and the first real pianist was Mozart's contemporary and rival, Muzio Clementi. His chief significance lies in his influence as a technician, for he opened the way to the modern style of play with its greater sonority and capacity for expression. Under him passage playing became an entirely new thing; deftness, lightness, and fluency were replaced by stupendous virtuosoship, which rested, nevertheless, on a full and solid tone. He is said to have been able to trill in octaves with one hand. He was necessary for the adequate interpretation of Beethoven, whose music is likely to be best understood by those who know that he, too, was a superb pianoforte player, fully up to the requirements which his last sonatas make upon technical skill as well as intellectual and emotional gifts.

[Sidenote: Beethoven's technique.]

[Sidenote: Expression supreme.]

Czerny, who was a pupil of Beethoven, has preserved a fuller account of that great composer's art as a player than we have of any of his predecessors. He describes his technique as tremendous, better than that of any virtuoso of his day. He was remarkably deft in connecting the full chords, in which he delighted, without the use of the pedal. His manner at the instrument was composed and quiet. He sat erect, without movement of the upper body, and only when his deafness compelled him to do so, in order to hear his own music, did he contract a habit of leaning forward. With an evident appreciation of the necessities of old-time music he had a great admiration for clean fingering, especially in fugue playing, and he objected to the use of Cramer's studies in the instruction of his nephew by Czerny because they led to what he called a "sticky" style of play, and failed to bring out crisp staccatos and a light touch. But it was upon expression that he insisted most of all when he taught.

[Sidenote: Music and emotion.]

More than anyone else it was Beethoven who brought music back to the purpose which it had in its first rude state, when it sprang unvolitionally from the heart and lips of primitive man. It became again a vehicle for the feelings. As such it was accepted by the romantic composers to whom he belongs as father, seer, and prophet, quite as intimately as he belongs to the classicists by reason of his adherence to form as an essential in music. To his contemporaries he appears as an image-breaker, but to the clearer vision of to-day he stands an unshakable barrier to lawless iconoclasm. Says Sir George Grove, quoting Mr. Edward Dannreuther, in the passages within the inverted commas:

[Sidenote: Beethoven a Romanticist.]

"That he was no wild radical altering for the mere pleasure of alteration, or in the mere search for originality, is evident from the length of time during which he abstained from publishing, or even composing works of pretension, and from the likeness which his early works possess to those of his predecessors. He began naturally with the forms which were in use in his days, and his alteration of them grew very gradually with the necessities of his expression. The form of the sonata is 'the transparent veil through which Beethoven seems to have looked at all music.' And the good points of that form he retained to the last--the 'triune symmetry of exposition, illustration, and repetition,' which that admirable method allowed and enforced--but he permitted himself a much greater liberty than his predecessors had done in the relationship of the keys of the different movements, and parts of movements, and in the proportion of the clauses and sections with which he built them up. In other words, he was less bound by the forms and musical rules, and more swayed by the thought which he had to express, and the directions which that thought took in his mind."

[Sidenote: Schumann and Chopin.]

It is scarcely to be wondered at that when men like Schumann and Chopin felt the full force of the new evangel which Beethoven had preached, they proceeded to carry the formal side of poetic expression, its vehicle, into regions unthought of before their time. The few old forms had now to give way to a large variety. In their work they proceeded from points that were far apart--Schumann's was literary, Chopin's political. In one respect the lists of their pieces which appear most frequently on recital programmes seem to hark back to the suites of two centuries ago--they are sets of short compositions grouped, either by the composer (as is the case with Schumann) or by the performer (as is the case with Chopin in the hands of Mr.

Paderewski). Such fantastic musical miniatures as Schumann's "Carnaval" and "Papillons" are eminently characteristic of the composer's intellectual and emotional nature, which in his university days had fallen under the spell of literary romanticism.

[Sidenote: Jean Paul's influence.]

[Sidenote: Schumann's inspirations.]

While ostensibly studying jurisprudence at Heidelberg, Schumann devoted seven hours a day to the pianoforte and several to Jean Paul. It was this writer who moulded not only Schumann's literary style in his early years, but also gave the bent which his creative activity in music took at the outset. To say little, but vaguely hint at much, was the rule which he adopted; to remain sententious in expression, but give the freest and most daring flight to his imagination, and spurn the conventional limitations set by rule and custom, his ambition. Such fanciful and symbolical titles as "Flower, Fruit, and Thorn Pieces," "Titan," etc., which Jean Paul adopted for his singular mixtures of tale, rhapsody, philosophy, and satire, were bound to find an imitator in so ardent an apostle as young Schumann, and, therefore, we have such compositions as "Papillons," "Carnaval," "Kreisleriana," "Phantasiest 點 ke," and the rest. Almost always, it may be said, the pieces which make them up were composed under the poetical and emotional impulses derived from literature, then grouped and named. To understand their poetic contents this must be known.

[Sidenote: Chopin's music.]

[Sidenote: Preludes.]

Chopin's fancy, on the other hand, found stimulation in the charm which, for him, lay in the tone of the pianoforte itself (to which he added a new loveliness by his manner of writing), as well as in the rhythms of the popular dances of his country. These dances he not only beautified as the old suite writers beautified their forms, but he utilized them as vessels which he filled with feeling, not all of which need be accepted as healthy, though much of it is. As to his titles, "Preludes" is purely an arbitrary designation for compositions which are equally indefinite in form and character; Niecks compares them very aptly to a portfolio full of drawings "in all stages of advancement--finished and unfinished, complete and incomplete compositions, sketches and mere memoranda, all mixed indiscriminately together." So, too, they appeared to Schumann: "They are sketches, commencements of studies, or, if you will, ruins, single eagle-wings, all strangely mixed together." Nevertheless some of them are marvellous soul-pictures.

[Sidenote: Etudes.]

[Sidenote: Nocturnes.]

The "Etudes" are studies intended to develop the technique of the pianoforte in the line of the composer's discoveries, his method of playing extended arpeggios, contrasted rhythms, progressions in thirds and octaves, etc., but still they breathe poetry and sometimes passion. Nocturne is an arbitrary, but expressive, title for a short composition of a dreamy, contemplative, or even elegiac, character. In many of his nocturnes Chopin is the adored sentimentalist of boarding-school misses. There is poppy in them and seductive poison for which Niecks sensibly prescribes Bach and Beethoven as antidotes. The term ballad has been greatly abused in literature, and in music is intrinsically unmeaning. Chopin's four Ballades have one feature in common--they are written in triple time; and they are among his finest inspirations.

[Sidenote: The Polonaise.]

Chopin's dances are conventionalized, and do not all speak the idiom of the people who created their forms, but their original characteristics ought to be known. The Polonaise was the stately dance of the Polish nobility, more a march or procession than a dance, full of gravity and courtliness, with an imposing and majestic rhythm in triple time that tends to emphasize the second beat of the measure, frequently syncopating it and accentuating the second half of the first beat:

[Music illustration]

[Sidenote: The Mazurka.]

National color comes out more clearly in his Mazurkas. Unlike the Polonaise this was the dance of the common people, and even as conventionalized and poetically refined by Chopin there is still in the Mazurka some of the rude vigor which lies in its propulsive rhythm:

[Sidenote: The Krakowiak.]

The Krakowiak (French Cracovienne, Mr. Paderewski has a fascinating specimen in his "Humoresques de Concert," op. 14) is a popular dance indigenous to the district of Cracow, whence its name. Its rhythmical elements are these:

[Sidenote: Idiomatic music.]

[Sidenote: Content higher than idiom.]

In the music of this period there is noticeable a careful attention on the part of the composers to the peculiarities of the pianoforte. No music, save perhaps that of Liszt, is so idiomatic. Frequently in Beethoven the content of the music seems too great for the medium of expression; we feel that the thought would have had better expression had the master used the orchestra instead of the pianoforte. We may well pause a moment to observe the development of the instrument and its technique from then till now, but as condemnation has already been pronounced against excessive admiration of technique for technique's sake, so now I would first utter a warning against our appreciation of the newer charm. "Idiomatic of the pianoforte" is a good enough phrase and a useful, indeed, but there is danger that if abused it may bring something like discredit to the instrument. It would be a pity if music, which contains the loftiest attributes of artistic beauty, should fail of appreciation simply because it had been observed that the pianoforte is not the most convenient, appropriate, or effective vehicle for its publication--a pity for the pianoforte, for therein would lie an exemplification of its imperfection. So, too, it would be a pity if the opinion should gain ground that music which had been clearly designed to meet the nature of the instrument was for that reason good pianoforte music, i.e., "idiomatic" music, irrespective of its content.

[Sidenote: Development of the pianoforte.]

In Beethoven's day the pianoforte was still a feeble instrument compared with the grand of to-day. Its capacities were but beginning to be appreciated. Beethoven had to seek and invent effects which now are known to every amateur. The instrument which the English manufacturer Broadwood presented to him in 1817 had a compass of six octaves, and was a whole octave wider in range than Mozart's pianoforte. In 1793 Clementi extended the key-board to five and a half octaves; six and a half octaves were reached in 1811, and seven in 1851. Since 1851 three notes have been added without material improvement to the instrument. This extension of compass, however, is far from being the most important improvement since the classic period. The growth in power, sonority, and tonal brilliancy has been much more marked, and of it Liszt made striking use.

[Sidenote: The Pedals.]

[Sidenote: Shifting pedal.]

[Sidenote: Damper pedal.]

Very significant, too, in their relation to the development of the music, were the invention and improvement of the pedals. The shifting pedal was invented by a Viennese maker named Stein, who first applied it to an instrument which he named "Saiten-harmonika." Before then soft effects were obtained by interposing a bit of felt between the hammers and the strings, as may still be seen in old square pianofortes. The shifting pedal, or soft pedal as it is popularly called, moves the key-board and action so that the hammer strikes only one or two of the unison strings, leaving the other to vibrate sympathetically. Beethoven was the first to appreciate the possibilities of this effect (see the slow movement of his concerto in G major and his last sonatas), but after him came Schumann and Chopin, and brought pedal manipulation to perfection, especially that of the damper pedal. This is popularly called the loud pedal, and the vulgarest use to which it can be put is to multiply the volume of tone. It was Chopin who showed its capacity for sustaining a melody and enriching the color effects by releasing the strings from the dampers and utilizing the ethereal sounds which rise from the strings when they vibrate sympathetically.

[Sidenote: Liszt.]

[Sidenote: A dual character.]

It is no part of my purpose to indulge in criticism of composers, but something of the kind is made unavoidable by the position assigned to Liszt in our pianoforte recitals. He is relied upon to provide a scintillant close. The pianists, then, even those who are his professed admirers, are responsible if he is set down in our scheme as the exemplar of the technical cult. Technique having its unquestioned value, we are bound to admire the marvellous gifts which enabled Liszt practically to sum up all the possibilities of pianoforte mechanism in its present stage of construction, but we need not look with unalloyed gratitude upon his influence as a composer. There were, I fear, two sides to Liszt's artistic character as well as his moral. I believe he had in him a touch of charlatanism as well as a magnificent amount of artistic sincerity-- just as he blended a laxity of moral ideas with a profound religious mysticism. It would have been strange indeed, growing up as he did in the whited sepulchre of Parisian salon life, if he had not accustomed himself to sacrifice a little of the soul of art for the sake of vainglory, and a little of its poetry and feeling to make display of those dazzling digital feats which he invented. But, be it said to his honor, he never played mountebank tricks in the presence of the masters whom he revered. It was when he approached the music of Beethoven that he sank all thought of self and rose to a peerless height as an interpreting artist.

[Sidenote: Liszt's Hungarian Rhapsodies.]

[Sidenote: Gypsies and Magyars.]

Liszt's place as a composer of original music has not yet been determined, but as a transcriber of the music of others the givers of pianoforte recitals keep him always before us. The showy Hungarian Rhapsodies with which the majority of pianoforte recitals end are, however, more than mere transcriptions. They are constructed out of the folk-songs of the Magyars, and in their treatment the composer has frequently reproduced the characteristic performances which they receive at the hands of the Gypsies from whom he learned them. This fact and the belief to which Liszt gave currency in his book

"Des Bohiens et de leur musique en Hongrie" have given rise to the almost universal belief that the Magyar melodies are of Gypsy origin. This belief is erroneous. The Gypsies have for centuries been the musical practitioners of Hungary, but they are not the composers of the music of the Magyars, though they have put a marked impress not only on the melodies, but also on popular taste. The Hungarian folk-songs are a perfect reflex of the national character of the Magyars, and some have been traced back centuries in their literature. Though their most marked melodic peculiarity, the frequent use of a minor scale containing one or even two superfluous seconds, as thus:

[Sidenote: Magyar scales.]

may be said to belong to Oriental music as a whole (and the Magyars are Orientals), the songs have a rhythmical peculiarity which is a direct product of the Magyar language. This peculiarity consists of a figure in which the emphasis is shifted from the strong to the weak part by making the first take only a fraction of the time of the second, thus:

[Sidenote: The Scotch snap.]

[Sidenote: Gypsy epics.]

In Scottish music this rhythm also plays a prominent part, but there it falls into the beginning of a measure, whereas in Hungarian it forms the middle or end. The result is an effect of syncopation which is peculiarly forceful. There is an indubitable Oriental relic in the profuse embellishments which the Gypsies weave around the Hungarian melodies when playing them; but the fact that they thrust the same embellishments upon Spanish and Russian music, in fact upon all the music which they play, indicates plainly enough that the impulse to do so is native to them, and has nothing to do with the national taste of the countries for which they provide music. Liszt's confessed purpose in writing the Hungarian Rhapsodies was to create what he called "Gypsy epics." He had gathered a large number of the melodies without a definite purpose, and was pondering what to do with them, when it occurred to him that

"These fragmentary, scattered melodies were the wandering, floating, nebulous part of a great whole, that they fully answered the conditions for the production of an harmonious unity which would comprehend the very flower of their essential properties, their most unique beauties," and "might be united in one homogeneous body, a complete work, its divisions to be so arranged that each song would form at once a whole and a part, which might be severed from the rest and be examined and enjoyed by and for itself; but which would, none the less, belong to the whole through the close affinity of subject matter, the similarity of its inner nature and unity in development."[D]

[Sidenote: The Czardas.]

The basis of Liszt's Rhapsodies being thus distinctively national, he has in a manner imitated in their character and tempo the dual character of the Hungarian national dance, the Czardas, which consists of two movements, a Lassu, or slow movement, followed by a Friss. These alternate at the will of the dancer, who gives a sign to the band when he wishes to change from one to the other.

FOOTNOTES:

[D] Weitzmann, "Geschichte des Clavierspiels," p. 197.

VII

At the Opera

[Sidenote: Instability of taste.]

[Sidenote: The age of operas.]

Popular taste in respect of the opera is curiously unstable. It is surprising that the canons of judgment touching it have such feeble and fleeting authority in view of the popularity of the art-form and the despotic hold which it has had on fashion for two centuries. No form of popular entertainment is acclaimed so enthusiastically as a new opera by an admired composer; none forgotten so quickly. For the spoken drama we go back to Shakespeare in the vernacular, and, on occasions, we revive the masterpieces of the Attic poets who flourished more than two millenniums ago; but for opera we are bounded by less than a century, unless occasional performances of Gluck's "Orfeo" and Mozart's "Figaro," "Don Giovanni," and "Magic Flute" be counted as submissions to popular demand, which, unhappily, we know they are not. There is no one who has attended the opera for twenty-five years who might not bewail the loss of operas from the current list which appealed to his younger fancy as works of real loveliness. In the season of 1895-96 the audiences at the Metropolitan Opera House in New York heard twenty-six different operas. The oldest were Gluck's "Orfeo" and Beethoven's "Fidelio," which had a single experimental representation each. After them in seniority came Donizetti's "Lucia di Lammermoor," which is sixty-one years old, and has overpassed the average age of "immortal" operas by from ten to twenty years, assuming Dr. Hanslick's calculation to be correct.

[Sidenote: Decimation of the operatic list.]

[Sidenote: Dependence on singers.]

The composers who wrote operas for the generation that witnessed Adelina Patti's debut at the Academy of Music, in New York, were Bellini, Donizetti, Verdi, and Meyerbeer. Thanks to his progressive genius, Verdi is still alive on the stage, though nine-tenths of the operas which made his fame and fortune have already sunk into oblivion; Meyerbeer, too, is still a more or less potent factor with his "Huguenots," which, like "Lucia," has endured from ten to twenty years longer than the average "immortal;" but the continued existence of Bellini and Donizetti seems to be as closely bound up with that of two or three singers as was Meleager's life with the burning billet which his mother snatched from the flames. So far as the people of London and New York are concerned whether or not they shall hear Donizetti more, rests with Mesdames Patti and Melba, for Donizetti spells "Lucia;" Bellini pleads piteously in "Sonnambula," but only Madame Nevada will play the mediator between him and our stiff-necked generation.

[Sidenote: An unstable art-form.]

[Sidenote: Carelessness of the public.]

[Sidenote: Addison's criticism.]

[Sidenote: Indifference to the words.]

Opera is a mixed art-form and has ever been, and perhaps must ever be, in a state of flux, subject to the changes of taste in music, the drama, singing, acting, and even politics and morals; but in one particular the public has shown no change for a century and a half, and it is not quite clear why this has not given greater fixity to popular appreciation. The people of to-day are as blithely indifferent to the fact that their operas are all presented in a foreign tongue as they were two centuries ago in England. The influence of Wagner has done much to stimulate a serious attitude toward the lyric drama, but this is seldom found outside of the audiences in attendance on German representations. The devotees of the Latin exotic, whether it blend French or Italian (or both, as is the rule in New York and London) with its melodic perfume, enjoy the music and ignore the words with the same nonchalance that Addison made merry over. Addison proves to have been a poor prophet. The great-grandchildren of his contemporaries are not at all curious to know "why their forefathers used to sit together like an audience of foreigners in their own country, and to hear whole plays acted before them in a tongue which they did not understand." What their great-grandparents did was also done by their grandparents and their parents, and may be done by their children, grandchildren, and great-grandchildren after them, unless Englishmen and Americans shall take to heart the lessons which Wagner essayed to teach his own people. For the present, though we have abolished many absurdities which grew out of a conception of opera that was based upon the simple, sensuous delight which singing gave, the charm of music is still supreme, and we can sit out an opera without giving a thought to the words uttered by the singers. The popular attitude is fairly represented by that of Boileau, when he went to hear "Atys" and requested the box-keeper to put him in a place where he could hear Lully's music, which he loved, but not Quinault's words, which he despised.

[Sidenote: Past and present.]

It is interesting to note that in this respect the condition of affairs in London in the early part of the eighteenth century, which seemed so monstrously diverting to Addison, was like that in Hamburg in the latter part of the seventeenth, and in New York at the end of the nineteenth. There were three years in London when Italian and English were mixed in the operatic representations.

"The king or hero of the play generally spoke in Italian and his slaves answered him in English; the lover frequently made his court and gained the heart of his princess in a language which she did not understand."

[Sidenote: Polyglot opera.]

At length, says Addison, the audience got tired of understanding half the opera, "and to ease themselves entirely of the fatigue of thinking, so ordered it that the whole opera was performed in an unknown tongue."

[Sidenote: Perversions of texts.]

There is this difference, however, between New York and London and Hamburg at the period referred to: while the operatic ragout was compounded of Italian and English in London, Italian and German in Hamburg, the ingredients here are Italian, French, and German, with no admixture of the vernacular. Strictly speaking, our case is more desperate than that of our foreign predecessors, for the development of the lyric drama has lifted its verbal and dramatic elements into a position not dreamed of two hundred years ago. We might endure with equanimity to hear the chorus sing

[Sidenote: "Robert le Diable."]

"_La soupe aux choux se fait dans la marmite, Dans la marmite on fait la soupe aux choux_"

at the beginning of "Robert le Diable," as tradition says used to be done in Paris, but we surely ought to rise in rebellion when the chorus of guards change their muttered comments on Pizarro's furious aria in "Fidelio" from

[Sidenote: "Fidelio."]

"Er spricht von Tod und Wunde!"

to

"Er spricht vom todten Hunde!"

as is a prevalent custom among the irreverent choristers of Germany.

Addison confesses that he was often afraid when seeing the Italian performers "chattering in the vehemence of action," that they were calling the audience names and abusing them among themselves. I do not know how to measure the morals and manners of our Italian singers against those of Addison's time, but I do know that many of the things which they say before our very faces for their own diversion are not complimentary to our intelligence. I hope I have a proper respect for Mr. Gilbert's "bashful young potato," but I do not think it right while we are sympathizing with the gentle passion of Siebel to have his representative bring an offering of flowers and, looking us full in the face, sing:

"Le patate d'amor, O cari fior!"

[Sidenote: "Faust."]

[Sidenote: Porpora's "Credo."]

It isn't respectful, and it enables the cynics of to-day to say, with the poetasters and fiddlers of Addison's day, that nothing is capable of being well set to music that is not nonsense. Operatic words were once merely stalking-horses for tunes, but that day is past. We used to smile at Brignoli's "Ah si! ah si! ah si!" which did service for any text in high passages; but if a composer should, for the accommodation of his music, change the wording of the creed into "Credo, non credo, non credo in unum Deum," as Porpora once did, we should all cry out for his excommunication.

As an art-form the opera has frequently been criticised as an absurdity, and it is doubtless owing to such a conviction that many people are equally indifferent to the language employed and the sentiments embodied in the words. Even so serious a writer as George Hogarth does not hesitate in his "Memoirs of the Opera" to defend this careless attitude.

[Sidenote: Are words unessential?]

"The words of an air are of small importance to the comprehension of the business of the piece," he says; "they merely express a sentiment, a reflection, a feeling; it is quite enough if their general import is known, and this may most frequently be gathered from the situation, aided by the character and expression of the music."

[Sidenote: "Il Trovatore."]

I, myself, have known an ardent lover of music who resolutely refused to look into a libretto because, being of a lively and imaginative temperament, she preferred to construct her own plots and put her own words in the mouths of the singers. Though a constant attendant on the opera, she never knew what "Il Trovatore" was about, which, perhaps, is not so surprising after all. Doubtless the play which she had fashioned in her own mind was more comprehensible than Verdi's medley of burnt children and asthmatic dance rhythms. Madame went so far as to condemn the German composers because they "follow too closely the sense of the words," whereas the Italians, "who are truly the musicians of nature, make the air and the words conform to each other only in a general way."

[Sidenote: The opera defended as an art-form.]

[Sidenote: The classic tragedy.]

Now the present generation has witnessed a revolution in operatic ideas which has lifted the poetical elements upon a plane not dreamed of when opera was merely a concert in costume, and it is no longer tolerable that it be set down as an absurdity. On the contrary, I believe that, looked at in the light thrown upon it by the history of the drama and the origin of music, the opera is completely justified as an art-form, and, in its best estate, is an entirely reasonable and highly effective entertainment. No mean place, surely, should be given in the estimation of the judicious to an art-form which aims in an equal degree to charm the senses, stimulate the emotions, and persuade the reason. This, the opera, or, perhaps I would better say the lyric drama, can be made to do as efficiently as the Greek tragedy did it, so far as the differences between the civilizations of ancient Hellas and the nineteenth century will permit. The Greek tragedy was the original opera, a fact which literary study would alone have made plain even if it were not clearly of record that it was an effort to restore the ancient plays in their integrity that gave rise to the Italian opera three centuries ago.

[Sidenote: Genesis of the Greek plays.]

Every school-boy knows now that the Hellenic plays were simply the final evolution of the dances with which the people of Hellas celebrated their religious festivals. At the rustic Bacchic feasts of the early Greeks they sang hymns in honor of the wine-god, and danced on goat-skins filled with wine. He who held his footing best on the treacherous surface carried home the wine as a reward. They contended in athletic games and songs for a goat, and from this circumstance scholars have surmised we have the word tragedy, which means "goat-song." The choric songs and dances grew in variety and beauty. Finally, somebody (tradition preserves the name of Thespis as the man) conceived the idea of introducing a simple dialogue between the strophes of the choric song. Generally this dialogue took the form of a recital of some story concerning the god whose festival was celebrating. Then when the dithyrambic song returned, it would either continue the narrative or comment on its ethical features.

[Sidenote: Mimicry and dress.]

The merry-makers, or worshippers, as one chooses to look upon them, manifested their enthusiasm by imitating the appearance as well as the actions of the god and his votaries. They smeared themselves with wine-lees, colored their bodies black and red, put on masks, covered themselves with the skins of beasts, enacted the parts of nymphs, fauns, and satyrs, those creatures of primitive fancy, half men and half goats, who were the representatives of natural sensuality untrammelled by conventionality.

[Sidenote: Melodrama.]

Next, somebody (Archilocus) sought to heighten the effect of the story or the dialogue by consorting it with instrumental music; and thus we find the germ of what musicians--not newspaper writers--call melodrama, in the very early stages of the drama's development. Gradually these simple rustic entertainments were taken in hand by the poets who drew on the legendary stores of the people for subjects, branching out from the doings of gods to the doings of god-like men, the popular heroes, and developed out of them the masterpieces of dramatic poetry which are still studied with amazement, admiration, and love.

[Sidenote: Factors in ancient tragedy.]

The dramatic factors which have been mustered in this outline are these:

1. The choric dance and song with a religious purpose.

2. Recitation and dialogue.

3. Characterization by means of imitative gestures--pantomime, that is--and dress.

4. Instrumental music to accompany the song and also the action.

[Sidenote: Operatic elements.]

[Sidenote: Words and music united.]

All these have been retained in the modern opera, which may be said to differ chiefly from its ancient model in the more important and more independent part which music plays in it. It will appear later in our study that the importance and independence achieved by one of the elements consorted in a work by nature composite, led the way to a revolution having for its object a restoration of something like the ancient drama. In this ancient drama and its precursor, the dithyrambic song and dance, is found a union of words and music which scientific investigation proves to be not only entirely natural but inevitable. In a general way most people are in the habit of speaking of music as the language of the emotions. The elements which enter into vocal music (of necessity the earliest form of music) are unvolitional products which we must conceive as co-existent with the beginnings of human life. Do they then antedate articulate speech? Did man sing before he spoke? I shall not quarrel with anybody who chooses so to put it.

[Sidenote: Physiology of singing.]

Think a moment about the mechanism of vocal music. Something occurs to stir up your emotional nature--a great joy, a great sorrow, a great fear; instantly, involuntarily, in spite of your efforts to prevent it, maybe, muscular actions set in which proclaim the emotion which fills you. The muscles and organs of the chest, throat, and mouth contract or relax in obedience to the emotion. You utter a cry, and according to the state of feeling which you are in, that cry has pitch, quality (timbre the singing teachers call it), and dynamic intensity. You attempt to speak, and no matter what the words you utter, the emotional drama playing on the stage of your heart is divulged.

[Sidenote: Herbert Spencer's laws.]

The man of science observes the phenomenon and formulates its laws, saying, for instance, as Herbert Spencer has said: "All feelings are muscular stimuli;" and, "Variations of voice are the physiological results of variations of feeling." It was the recognition of this extraordinary intimacy between the voice and the emotions which brought music all the world over into the service of religion, and provided the phenomenon, which we may still observe if we be but minded to do so, that mere tones have sometimes the sanctity of words, and must as little be changed as ancient hymns and prayers.

[Sidenote: Invention of Italian opera.]

[Sidenote: Musical declamation.]

The end of the sixteenth century saw a coterie of scholars, art-lovers, and amateur musicians in Florence who desired to re-establish the relationship which they knew had once existed between music and the drama. The revival of learning had made the classic tragedy dear to their hearts. They knew that in the olden time tragedy, of which the words only have come down to us, had been musical throughout. In their efforts to bring about an intimacy between dramatic poetry and music they found that nothing could be done with the polite music of their time. It was the period of highest development in ecclesiastical music, and the climax of artificiality. The professional musicians to whom they turned scorned their theories and would not help them; so they fell back on their own resources. They cut the Gordian knot and invented a new style of music, which they fancied was like that used by the ancients in their stage-plays. They abolished polyphony, or contrapuntal music, in everything except their choruses, and created a sort of musical declamation, using variations of pitch and harmonies built up on a simple bass to give emotional life to their words. In choosing their tones they were guided by observation of the vocal inflections produced in speech under stress of feeling, showing thus a recognition of the law which Herbert Spencer formulated two hundred and fifty years later.

[Sidenote: The music of the Florentine reformers.]

[Sidenote: The solo style, harmony, and declamation.]

[Sidenote: Fluent recitatives.]

The music which these men produced and admired sounds to us monotonous in the extreme, for what little melody there is in it is in the choruses, which they failed to emancipate from the ecclesiastical art, and which for that reason were as stiff and inelastic as the music which in their controversies with the musicians they condemned with vigor. Yet within their invention there lay an entirely new world of music. Out of it came the solo style, a song with instrumental accompaniment of a kind unknown to the church composers. Out of it, too, came harmony as an independent factor in music instead of an accident of the simultaneous flow of melodies; and out of it came declamation, which drew its life from the text. The recitatives which they wrote had the fluency of spoken words and were not retarded by melodic forms. The new style did not accomplish what its creators hoped for, but it gave birth to Italian opera and emancipated music in a large measure from the formalism that dominated it so long as it belonged exclusively to the composers for the church.

[Sidenote: Predecessors of Wagner.]

[Sidenote: Old operatic distinctions.]

[Sidenote: Opera buffa.]

[Sidenote: Opera seria.]

[Sidenote: Recitative.]

Detailed study of the progress of opera from the first efforts of the Florentines to Wagner's dramas would carry us too far afield to serve the purposes of this book. My aim is to fix the attitude proper, or at least useful, to the opera audience of to-day. The excursion into history which I have made has but the purpose to give the art-form a reputable standing in court, and to explain the motives which prompted the revolution accomplished by Wagner. As to the elements which compose an opera, only those need particular attention which are illustrated in the current repertory. Unlike the opera audiences of two centuries ago, we are not required to distinguish carefully between the various styles of opera in order to understand why the composer adopted a particular manner, and certain fixed forms in each. The old distinctions between Opera seria, Opera buffa, and _Opera semiseria_ perplex us no more. Only because of the perversion of the time-honored Italian epithet buffa by the French mongrel _Opera bouffe is it necessary to explain that the classic Opera buffa_ was a polite comedy, whose musical integument did not of necessity differ from that of Opera seria except in this-- that the dialogue was carried on in "dry" recitative (recitativo secco, or parlante) in the former, and a more measured declamation with orchestral accompaniment (recitativo stromentato) in the latter. So far as subject-matter was concerned the classic distinction between tragedy and comedy served. The dry recitative was supported by chords played by a double-bass and harpsichord or pianoforte. In London, at a later period, for reasons of doubtful validity, these chords came to be played on a double-bass and violoncello, as we occasionally hear them to-day.

[Sidenote: Opera semiseria.]

[Sidenote: "Don Giovanni."]

Shakespeare has taught us to accept an infusion of the comic element in plays of a serious cast, but Shakespeare was an innovator, a Romanticist, and, measured by old standards, his dramas are irregular. The Italians, who followed classic models, for a reason amply explained by the genesis of the art-form, rigorously excluded comedy from serious operas, except as intermezzi, until they hit upon a third classification, which they called Opera semiseria, in which a serious subject was enlivened with comic episodes. Our dramatic tastes being grounded in Shakespeare, we should be inclined to put down "Don Giovanni" as a musical tragedy; or, haunted by the Italian terminology, as Opera semiseria; but Mozart calls it Opera buffa, more in deference to the librettist's work, I fancy, than his own, for, as I have suggested elsewhere,[E] the musician's imagination in the fire of composition went far beyond the conventional fancy of the librettist in the finale of that most wonderful work.

[Sidenote: An Opera buffa.]

[Sidenote: French Grand Opera.]

[Sidenote: Opera comique.]

[Sidenote: "Mignon."]

[Sidenote: "Faust."]

It is well to remember that "Don Giovanni" is an Opera buffa when watching the buffooneries of Leporello, for that alone justifies them. The French have Grand Opera, in which everything is sung to orchestra accompaniment, there being neither spoken dialogue nor dry recitative, and Opera comique, in which the dialogue is spoken. The latter corresponds with the honorable German term Singspiel, and one will not go far astray if he associate both terms with the English operas of Wallace and Balfe, save that the French and Germans have generally been more deft in bridging over the chasm between speech and song than their British rivals. Opera comique has another characteristic, its denouement must be happy. Formerly the Theatre national de l'Opera-Comique_ in Paris was devoted exclusively to Opera comique as thus defined (it has since abolished the distinction and Grand Opera may be heard there now), and, therefore, when Ambroise Thomas brought forward his "Mignon," Goethe's story was found to be changed so that Mignon recovered and was married to Wilhelm Meister at the end. The Germans are seldom pleased with the transformations which their literary masterpieces are forced to undergo at the hands of French librettists. They still refuse to call Gounod's "Faust" by that name; if you wish to hear it in Germany you must go to the theatre when "Margarethe" is performed. Naturally they fell indignantly afoul of "Mignon," and to placate them we have a second finale, a denouement allemand, provided by the authors, in which Mignon dies as she ought.

[Sidenote: Grosse Oper.]

[Sidenote: Comic opera and operetta.]

[Sidenote: Opera bouffe.]

[Sidenote: Romantic operas.]

Of course the Grosse Oper of the Germans is the French Grand Opera and the English grand opera--but all the English terms are ambiguous, and everything that is done in Covent Garden in London or the Metropolitan Opera House in New York is set down as "grand opera," just as the vilest imitations of the French vaudevilles or English farces with music are called "comic operas." In its best estate, say in the delightful works of Gilbert and Sullivan, what is designated as comic opera ought to be called operetta, which is a piece in which the forms of grand opera are imitated, or travestied, the dialogue is spoken, and the purpose of the play is to satirize a popular folly. Only in method, agencies, and scope does such an operetta (the examples of Gilbert and Sullivan are in mind) differ from comedy in its best conception, as a dramatic composition which aims to "chastise manners with a smile" ("Ridendo castigat mores"). Its present degeneracy, as illustrated in the Opera bouffe of the French and the concoctions of the would-be imitators of Gilbert and Sullivan, exemplifies little else than a pursuit far into the depths of the method suggested by a friend to one of Lully's imitators who had expressed a fear that a ballet written, but not yet performed, would fail. "You must lengthen the dances and shorten the ladies' skirts," he said. The Germans make another distinction based on the subject chosen for the story. Spohr's "Jessonda," Weber's "Freischez," "Oberon," and "Euryanthe," Marschner's "Vampyr," "Templer und J廛 in," and "Hans Heiling" are "Romantic" operas. The significance of this classification in operatic literature may be learned from an effort which I have made in another chapter to discuss the terms Classic and Romantic as applied to music. Briefly stated, the operas mentioned are put in a class by themselves (and their imitations with them) because their plots were drawn from the romantic legends of the Middle Ages, in which the institutions of chivalry, fairy lore, and supernaturalism play a large part.

[Sidenote: Modern designations.]

[Sidenote: German opera and Wagner.]

These distinctions we meet in reading about music. As I have intimated, we do not concern ourselves much with them now. In New York and London the people speak of Italian, English, and German opera, referring generally to the language employed in the performance. But there is also in the use of the terms an underlying recognition of differences in ideals of performance. As all operas sung in the regular seasons at Covent Garden and the Metropolitan Opera House are popularly spoken of as Italian operas, so German opera popularly means Wagner's lyric dramas, in the first instance, and a style of performance which grew out of Wagner's influence in the second. As compared with Italian opera, in which the principal singers are all and the ensemble nothing, it means, mayhap, inferior vocalists but better actors in the principal parts, a superior orchestra and chorus, and a more conscientious effort on the part of conductor, stage manager, and artists, from first to last, to lift the general effect above the conventional level which has prevailed for centuries in the Italian opera houses.

[Sidenote: Wagner's "Musikdrama."]

[Sidenote: Modern Italian terminology.]

In terminology, as well as in artistic aim, Wagner's lyric dramas round out a cycle that began with the works of the Florentine reformers of the sixteenth century. Wagner called his later operas Musikdramen, wherefore he was soundly abused and ridiculed by his critics. When the Italian opera first appeared it was called _Dramma per musica, or Melodramma, or Tragedia per musica_, all of which terms stand in Italian for the conception that Musikdrama stands for in German. The new thing had been in existence for half a century, and was already on the road to the degraded level on which we shall find it when we come to the subject of operatic singing, before it came to be called Opera in musica, of which "opera" is an abbreviation. Now it is to be observed that the composers of all countries, having been taught to believe that the dramatic contents of an opera have some significance, are abandoning the vague term "opera" and following Wagner in his adoption of the principles underlying the original terminology. Verdi called his "Aida" an Opera in quattro atti, but his "Otello" he designated a lyric drama (Dramma lirico), his "Falstaff" a lyric comedy (Commedia lirica), and his example is followed by the younger Italian composers, such as Mascagni, Leoncavallo, and Puccini.

[Sidenote: Recitative.]

In the majority of the operas of the current list the vocal element illustrates an amalgamation of the archaic recitative and aria. The dry form of recitative is met with now only in a few of the operas which date back to the last century or the early years of the present. "Le Nozze di Figaro," "Don Giovanni," and "Il Barbiere di Siviglia" are the most familiar works in which it is employed, and in the second of these it is used only by the bearers of the comedy element. The dissolute Don chatters glibly in it with Zerlina, but when Donna Anna and Don Ottavio converse, it is in the _recitativo stromentato_.

[Sidenote: The object of recitative.]

[Sidenote: Defects of the recitative.]

[Sidenote: What it can do.]

In both forms recitative is the vehicle for promoting the action of the play, preparing its incidents, and paving the way for the situations and emotional states which are exploited, promulgated, and dwelt upon in the set music pieces. Its purpose is to maintain the play in an artificial atmosphere, so that the transition from dialogue to song may not be so abrupt as to disturb the mood of the listener. Of all the factors in an opera, the dry recitative is the most monotonous. It is not music, but speech about to break into music. Unless one is familiar with Italian and desirous of following the conversation, which we have been often told is not necessary to the enjoyment of an opera, its everlasting use of stereotyped falls and intervallic turns, coupled with the strumming of arpeggioed cadences on the pianoforte (or worse, double-bass and violoncello), makes it insufferably wearisome to the listener. Its expression is fleeting--only for the moment. It lacks the sustained tones and structural symmetry essential to melody, and therefore it cannot sustain a mood. It makes efficient use of only one of the fundamental factors of vocal music--variety of pitch--and that in a rudimentary way. It is specifically a product of the Italian language, and best adapted to comedy in that language. Spoken with the vivacity native to it in the drama, dry recitative is an impossibility in English. It is only in the more measured and sober gait proper to oratorio that we can listen to it in the vernacular without thought of incongruity. Yet it may be made most admirably to preserve the characteristics of conversation, and even illustrate Spencer's theory of the origin of music. Witness the following brief example from "Don Giovanni," in which the vivacity of the master is admirably contrasted with the lumpishness of his servant:

[Sidenote: An example from Mozart.]

DON GIOVANNI. LEPORELLO. Le-po-rel-lo, o-ve sei? Son qui per Le-po-rel-lo, where are you? I'm here and

D.G. LEP. dis-gra-zi-a! e vo-i? Son qui. Chi ?more's the pit-y! and you, Sir? Here too. Who's

D.G. mor-to, voi, o il vec-chio? Che do- been killed, you or the old one? What a

LEP. man-da da bes-tia! il vec-chio. Bra-vo! ques-tion, you boo-by! the old one. Bra-vo!]

[Sidenote: Its characteristics.]

Of course it is left to the intelligence and taste of the singers to bring out the effects in a recitative, but in this specimen it ought to be noted how sluggishly the disgruntled Leporello replies to the brisk question of Don Giovanni, how correct is the rhetorical pause in "you, or the old one?" and the greater sobriety which comes over the manner of the Don as he thinks of the murder just committed, and replies, "the old one."

[Sidenote: Recitative of some sort necessary.]

[Sidenote: The speaking voice in opera.]

I am strongly inclined to the belief that in one form or the other, preferably the accompanied, recitative is a necessary integer in the operatic sum. That it is possible to accustom one's self to the change alternately from speech to song we know from the experiences made with German, French, and English operas, but these were not true lyric dramas, but dramas with incidental music. To be a real lyric drama an opera ought to be musical throughout, the voice being maintained from beginning to end on an exalted plane. The tendency to drop into the speaking voice for the sake of dramatic effect shown by some tragic singers does not seem to me commendable. Wagner relates with enthusiasm how Madame Schroeder-Devrient in "Fidelio" was wont to give supreme emphasis to the phrase immediately preceding the trumpet signal in the dungeon scene ("Another step, and you are dead!") by speaking the last word "with an awful accent of despair." He then comments:

"The indescribable effect of this manifested itself to all like an agonizing plunge from one sphere into another, and its sublimity consisted in this, that with lightning quickness a glimpse was given to us of the nature of both spheres, of which one was the ideal, the other the real."

[Sidenote: Wagner and Schroeder-Devrient.]

I have heard a similar effect produced by Herr Niemann and Madame Lehmann, but could not convince myself that it was not an extremely venturesome experiment. Madame Schroeder-Devrient saw the beginning of the modern methods of dramatic expression, and it is easy to believe that a sudden change like that so well defined by Wagner, made with her sweeping voice and accompanied by her plastic and powerful acting, was really thrilling; but, I fancy, nevertheless, that only Beethoven and the intensity of feeling which pervades the scene saved the audience from a disturbing sense of the incongruity of the performance.

[Sidenote: Early forms.]

[Sidenote: The dialogue of the Florentines.]

The development which has taken place in the recitative has not only assisted in elevating opera to the dignity of a lyric drama by saving us from alternate contemplation of the two spheres of ideality and reality, but has also made the factor itself an eloquent vehicle of dramatic expression. Save that it had to forego the help of the instruments beyond a mere harmonic support, the _stilo rappresentativo, or musica parlante_, as the Florentines called their musical dialogue, approached the sustained recitative which we hear in the oratorio and grand opera more closely than it did the recitative secco. Ever and anon, already in the earliest works (the "Eurydice" of Rinuccini as composed by both Peri and Caccini) there are passages which sound like rudimentary melodies, but are charged with vital dramatic expression. Note the following phrase from Orpheus's monologue on being left in the infernal regions by Venus, from Peri's opera, performed A.D. 1600, in honor of the marriage of Maria de' Medici to Henry IV. of France:

[Sidenote: An example from Peri.]

[Music illustration:

E voi, deh per pie-t? del mio mar-ti-re Che nel mi-se-ro cor di-mo-ra e-ter-no, La-cri-ma-te al mio pian-to om-bre d'in-fer-no!]

[Sidenote: Development of the arioso.]

[Sidenote: The aria supplanted.]

[Sidenote: Music and action.]

Out of this style there grew within a decade something very near the arioso, and for all the purposes of our argument we may accept the melodic devices by which Wagner carries on the dialogue of his operas as an uncircumscribed arioso superimposed upon a foundation of orchestral harmony; for example, Lohengrin's address to the swan, Elsa's account of her dream. The greater melodiousness of the recitativo stromentato, and the aid of the orchestra when it began to assert itself as a factor of independent value, soon enabled this form of musical conversation to become a reflector of the changing moods and passions of the play, and thus the value of the aria, whether considered as a solo, or in its composite form as duet, trio, quartet, or ensemble, was lessened. The growth of the accompanied recitative naturally brought with it emancipation from the tyranny of the classical aria. Wagner's reform had nothing to do with that emancipation, which had been accomplished before him, but went, as we shall see presently, to a liberation of the composers from all the formal dams which had clogged the united flow of action and music. We should, however, even while admiring the achievements of modern composers in blending these elements (and I know of no more striking illustration than the scene of the fat knight's discomfiture in Ford's house in Verdi's "Falstaff") bear in mind that while we may dream of perfect union between words and music, it is not always possible that action and music shall go hand in hand. Let me repeat what once I wrote in a review of Cornelius's opera, "Der Barbier von Bagdad:"[F]

[Sidenote: How music can replace incident.]

"After all, of the constituents of an opera, action, at least that form of it usually called incident, is most easily spared. Progress in feeling, development of the emotional element, is indeed essential to variety of musical utterance, but nevertheless all great operas have demonstrated that music is more potent and eloquent when proclaiming an emotional state than while seeking to depict progress toward such a state. Even in the dramas of Wagner the culminating musical moments are predominantly lyrical, as witness the love-duet in 'Tristan,' the close of 'Das Rheingold,' Siegmund's song, the love-duet, and Wotan's farewell in 'Die Walke,' the forest scene and final duet in 'Siegfried,' and the death of Siegfried in 'Die Gasterd merung.' It is in the nature of music that this should be so. For the drama which plays on the stage of the heart, music is a more truthful language than speech; but it can stimulate movement and prepare the mind for an incident better than it can accompany movement and incident. Yet music that has a high degree of emotional expressiveness, by diverting attention from externals to the play of passion within the breasts of the persons can sometimes make us forget the paucity of incident in a play. 'Tristan und Isolde' is a case in point. Practically, its outward action is summed up in each of its three acts by the same words: Preparation for a meeting of the ill-starred lovers; the meeting. What is outside of this is mere detail; yet the effect of the tragedy upon a listener is that of a play surcharged with pregnant occurrence. It is the subtle alchemy of music that transmutes the psychological action of the tragedy into dramatic incident."

[Sidenote: Set forms not to be condemned.]

[Sidenote: Wagner's influence.]

[Sidenote: His orchestra.]

[Sidenote: Vocal feats.]

For those who hold such a view with me it will be impossible to condemn pieces of set forms in the lyric drama. Wagner still represents his art-work alone, but in the influence which he exerted upon contemporaneous composers in Italy and France, as well as Germany, he is quite as significant a figure as he is as the creator of the Musikdrama. The operas which are most popular in our Italian and French repertories are those which benefited by the liberation from formalism and the exaltation of the dramatic idea which he preached and exemplified--such works as Gounod's "Faust," Verdi's "Aida" and "Otello," and Bizet's "Carmen." With that emancipation there came, as was inevitable, new conceptions of the province of dramatic singing as well as new convictions touching the mission of the orchestra. The instruments in Wagner's latter-day works are quite as much as the singing actors the expositors of the dramatic idea, and in the works of the other men whom I have mentioned they speak a language which a century ago was known only to the orchestras of Gluck and Mozart with their comparatively limited, yet eloquent, vocabulary. Coupled with praise for the wonderful art of Mesdames Patti and Melba (and I am glad to have lived in their generation, though they do not represent my ideal in dramatic singing), we are accustomed to hear lamentations over the decay of singing. I have intoned such jeremiads myself, and I do not believe that music is suffering from a greater want to-day than that of a more thorough training for singers. I marvel when I read that Senesino sang cadences of fifty seconds' duration; that Ferri with a single breath could trill upon each note of two octaves, ascending and descending, and that La Bastardella's art was equal to a perfect performance (perfect in the conception of her day) of a flourish like this:

[Sidenote: La Bastardella's flourish.]

[Sidenote: Character of the opera a century and a half ago.]

[Sidenote: Music and dramatic expression.]

I marvel, I say, at the skill, the gifts, and the training which could accomplish such feats, but I would not have them back again if they were to be employed in the old service. When Senesino, Farinelli, Sassarelli, Ferri, and their tribe dominated the stage, it strutted with sexless Agamemnons and Cæsars. Telemachus, Darius, Nero, Cato, Alexander, Scipio, and Hannibal ran around on the boards as languishing lovers, clad in humiliating disguises, singing woful arias to their mistress's eyebrows--arias full of trills and scales and florid ornaments, but void of feeling as a problem in Euclid. Thanks very largely to German influences, the opera is returning to its original purposes. Music is again become a means of dramatic expression, and the singers who appeal to us most powerfully are those who are best able to make song subserve that purpose, and who to that end give to dramatic truthfulness, to effective elocution, and to action the attention which mere voice and beautiful utterance received in the period which is called the Golden Age of singing, but which was the Leaden Age of the lyric drama.

[Sidenote: Singers heard in New York.]

For seventy years the people of New York, scarcely less favored than those of London, have heard nearly all the great singers of Europe. Let me talk about some of them, for I am trying to establish some ground on which my readers may stand when they try to form an estimate of the singing which they are privileged to hear in the opera houses of to-day. Madame Malibran was a member of the first Italian company that ever sang here. Madame Cinti-Damoreau came in 1844, Bosio in 1849, Jenny Lind in 1850, Sontag in 1853, Grisi in 1854, La Grange in 1855, Frezzolini in 1857, Piccolomini in 1858, Nilsson in 1870, Lucca in 1872, Titiens in 1876, Gerster in 1878, and Sembrich in 1883. I omit the singers of the German opera as belonging to a different category. Adelina Patti was always with us until she made her European debut in 1861, and remained abroad twenty years. Of the men who were the artistic associates of these prime donne, mention may be made of Mario, Benedetti, Corsi, Salvi, Ronconi, Formes, Brignoli, Amadeo, Coletti, and Campanini, none of whom, excepting Mario, was of first-class importance compared with the women singers.

[Sidenote: Grisi.]

[Sidenote: Jenny Lind.]

[Sidenote: Lilli Lehmann.]

Nearly all of these singers, even those still living and remembered by the younger generation of to-day, exploited their gifts in the operas of Rossini, Bellini, Donizetti, the early Verdi, and Meyerbeer. Grisi was acclaimed a great dramatic singer, and it is told of her that once in "Norma" she frightened the tenor who sang the part of Pollio by the fury of her acting. But measured by the standards of to-day, say that set by Calv?s Carmen, it must have been a simple age that could be impressed by the tragic power of anyone acting the part of Bellini's Druidical priestess. The surmise is strengthened by the circumstance that Madame Grisi created a sensation in "Il Trovatore" by showing signs of agitation in the tower scene, walking about the stage during Manrico's "Ah! che la morte ognora," as if she would fain discover the part of the castle where her lover was imprisoned. The chief charm of Jenny Lind in the memory of the older generation is the pathos with which she sang simple songs. Mendelssohn esteemed her greatly as a woman and artist, but he is quoted as once remarking to Chorley: "I cannot think why she always prefers to be in a bad theatre." Moscheles, recording his impressions of her in Meyerbeer's "Camp of Silesia" (now "L'席 oile du Nord"), reached the climax of his praise in the words: "Her song with the two concertante flutes is perhaps the most incredible feat in the way of bravura singing that can possibly be heard." She was credited, too, with fine powers as an actress; and that she possessed them can easily be believed, for few of the singers whom I have mentioned had so early and intimate an association with the theatre as she. Her repugnance to it in later life she attributed to a prejudice inherited from her mother. A vastly different heritage is disclosed by Madame Lehmann's devotion to the drama, a devotion almost akin to religion. I have known her to go into the scene-room of the Metropolitan Opera House in New York and search for mimic stumps and rocks with which to fit out a scene in "Siegfried," in which she was not even to appear. That, like her super-human work at rehearsals, was "for the good of the cause," as she expressed it.

[Sidenote: Sontag.]

Most amiable are the memories that cluster around the name of Sontag, whose career came to a grievous close by her sudden death in Mexico in 1854. She was a German, and the early part of her artistic life was influenced by German ideals, but it is said that only in the music of Mozart and Weber, which aroused in her strong national emotion, did she sing dramatically. For the rest she used her light voice, which had an extraordinary range, brilliancy, and flexibility, very much as Patti and Melba use their voices to-day--in mere unfeeling vocal display.

"She had an extensive soprano voice," says Hogarth; "not remarkable for power, but clear, brilliant, and singularly flexible; a quality which seems to have led her (unlike most German singers in general) to cultivate the most florid style, and even to follow the bad example set by Catalani, of seeking to convert her voice into an instrument, and to astonish the public by executing the violin variations on Rode's air and other things of that stamp."

[Sidenote: La Grange.]

[Sidenote: Piccolomini.]

[Sidenote: Adelina Patti.]

[Sidenote: Gerster.]

[Sidenote: Lucca and Nilsson.]

[Sidenote: Sembrich.]

Madame La Grange had a voice of wide compass, which enabled her to sing contralto roles as well as soprano, but I have never heard her dramatic powers praised. As for Piccolomini, read of her where you will, you shall find that she was "charming." She was lovely to look upon, and her acting in soubrette parts was fascinating. Until Melba came Patti was for thirty years peerless as a mere vocalist. She belongs, as did Piccolomini and Sontag, to the comic genre; so did Sembrich and Gerster, the latter of whom never knew it. I well remember how indignant she became on one occasion, in her first American season, at a criticism which I wrote of her Amina in "La Sonnambula," a performance which remains among my loveliest and most fragrant recollections. I had made use of Catalani's remark concerning Sontag:

"Son genre est petit, mais elle est unique dans son genre," and applied it to her style. She almost flew into a passion. "_Mon genre est grand!_" said she, over and over again, while Dr. Gardini, her husband, tried to pacify her. "Come to see my Marguerite next season." Now, Gounod's Marguerite does not quite belong to the heroic roles, though we can all remember how Lucca thrilled us by her intensity of action as well as of song, and how Madame Nilsson sent the blood out of our cheeks, though she did stride through the opera like a combination of the grande dame and Ary Scheffer's spirituelle pictures; but such as it is, Madame Gerster achieved a success of interest only, and that because of her strivings for originality. Sembrich and Gerster, when they were first heard in New York, had as much execution as Melba or Nilsson; but their voices had less emotional power than that of the latter, and less beauty than that of the former--beauty of the kind that might be called classic, since it is in no way dependent on feeling.

[Sidenote: Melba and Eames.]

[Sidenote: Calv?]

[Sidenote: Dramatic singers.]

[Sidenote: Jean de Reszke.]

[Sidenote: Edouard de Reszke]

Patti, Lucca, Nilsson, and Gerster sang in the operas in which Melba and Eames sing to-day, and though the standard of judgment has been changed in the last twenty-five years by the growth of German ideals, I can find no growth of potency in the performances of the representative women of Italian and French opera, except in the case of Madame Calv? For the development of dramatic ideals we must look to the singers of German affiliations or antecedents, Mesdames Materna, Lehmann, Sucher, and Nordica. As for the men of yesterday and to-day, no lover, I am sure, of the real lyric drama would give the declamatory warmth and gracefulness of pose and action which mark the performances of M. Jean de Reszke for a hundred of the high notes of Mario (for one of which, we are told, he was wont to reserve his powers all evening), were they never so lovely. Neither does the fine, resonant, equable voice of Edouard de Reszke or the finished style of

Plan leave us with curious longings touching the voices and manners of Lablache and Formes. Other times, other manners, in music as in everything else. The great singers of to-day are those who appeal to the taste of to-day, and that taste differs, as the clothes which we wear differ, from the style in vogue in the days of our ancestors.

[Sidenote: Wagner's operas.]

[Sidenote: Wagner's lyric dramas.]

[Sidenote: His theories.]

[Sidenote: The mission of music.]

[Sidenote: Distinctions abolished.]

[Sidenote: The typical phrases.]

[Sidenote: Characteristics of some motives.]

A great deal of confusion has crept into the public mind concerning Wagner and his works by the failure to differentiate between his earlier and later creations. No injustice is done the composer by looking upon his "Flying Dutchman," "Tannhauser," and "Lohengrin" as operas. We find the dramatic element lifted into noble prominence in "Tannhauser," and admirable freedom in the handling of the musical factors in "Lohengrin," but they must, nevertheless, be listened to as one would listen to the operas of Weber, Marschner, or Meyerbeer. They are, in fact, much nearer to the conventional operatic type than to the works which came after them, and were called Musikdramen. "Music drama" is an awkward phrase, and I have taken the liberty of substituting "lyric drama" for it, and as such I shall designate "Tristan und Isolde," "Die Meistersinger," "Der Ring des Nibelungen," and "Parsifal." In these works Wagner exemplified his reformatory ideas and accomplished a regeneration of the lyric drama, as we found it embodied in principle in the Greek tragedy and the _Dramma per musica_ of the Florentine scholars. Wagner's starting-point is, that in the opera music had usurped a place which did not belong to it.[G] It was designed to be a means and had become an end. In the drama he found a combination of poetry, music, pantomime, and scenery, and he held that these factors ought to co-operate on a basis of mutual dependence, the inspiration of all being dramatic expression. Music, therefore, ought to be subordinate to the text in which the dramatic idea is expressed, and simply serve to raise it to a higher power by giving it greater emotional life. So, also, it ought to vivify pantomime and accompany the stage pictures. In order that it might do all this, it had to be relieved of the shackles of formalism; only thus could it move with the same freedom as the other elements consorted with it in the drama. Therefore, the distinctions between recitative and aria were abolished, and an "endless melody" took the place of both. An exalted form of speech is borne along on a flood of orchestral music, which, quite as much as song, action, and scenery concerns itself with the exposition of the drama. That it may do this the agencies, spiritual as well as material, which are instrumental in the development of the play, are identified with certain melodic phrases, out of which the musical fabric is woven. These phrases are the much mooted, much misunderstood "leading motives"--typical phrases I call them. Wagner has tried to make them reflect the character or nature of the agencies with which he has associated them, and therefore we find the giants in the Niblung tetralogy symbolized in heavy, slowly moving, cumbersome phrases; the dwarfs have two phrases, one suggesting their occupation as smiths, by its hammering rhythm, and the other their intellectual habits, by its suggestion of brooding contemplativeness. I cannot go through the catalogue of the typical phrases which enter into the musical structure of the works which I have called lyric dramas as contra-distinguished from operas. They should, of course, be known to the student of Wagner, for thereby will he be helped to understand the poet-composer's purposes, but I would fain repeat the warning which I uttered twice in my "Studies in the Wagnerian Drama:"

[Sidenote: The phrases should be studied.]

"It cannot be too forcibly urged that if we confine our study of Wagner to the forms and names of the phrases out of which he constructs his musical fabric, we shall, at the last, have enriched our minds with a thematic catalogue and--nothing else. We shall remain guiltless of knowledge unless we learn something of the nature of those phrases by noting the attributes which lend them propriety and fitness, and can recognize, measurably at least, the reasons for their introduction and development. Those attributes give character and mood to the music constructed out of the phrases. If we are able to feel the mood, we need not care how the phrases which produce it have been labelled. If we do not feel the mood, we may memorize the whole thematic catalogue of Wolzogen and have our labor for our pains. It would be better to know nothing about the phrases, and content one's self with simple sensuous enjoyment than to spend one's time answering the baldest of all the riddles of Wagner's orchestra--'What am I playing now?'

[Sidenote: The question of effectiveness.]

"The ultimate question concerning the correctness or effectiveness of Wagner's system of composition must, of course, be answered along with the question: 'Does the composition, as a whole, touch the emotions, quicken the fancy, fire the imagination?' If it does these things, we may, to a great extent, if we wish, get along without the intellectual processes of reflection and comparison which are conditioned upon a recognition of the themes and their uses. But if we put aside this intellectual activity, we shall deprive ourselves, among other things, of the pleasures which it is the province of memory to give; and the exercise of memory is called for by music much more urgently than by any other art, because of its volatile nature and the role which repetition plays in it."

FOOTNOTES:

[E] "But no real student can have studied the score deeply, or listened discriminatingly to a good performance, without discovering that there is a tremendous chasm between the conventional aims of the Italian poet in the book of the opera and the work which emerged from the composer's profound imagination. Da Ponte contemplated a _dramma giocoso_; Mozart humored him until his imagination came within the shadow cast before by the catastrophe, and then he transformed the poet's comedy into a tragedy of crushing power. The climax of Da Ponte's ideal is reached in a picture of the dissolute Don wrestling in idle desperation with a host of spectacular devils, and finally disappearing through a trap, while fire bursts out on all sides, the thunders roll, and Leporello gazes on the scene, crouched in a comic attitude of terror, under the table. Such a picture satisfied the tastes of the public of his time, and that public found nothing incongruous in a return to the scene immediately afterwards of all the characters save the reprobate, who had gone to his reward, to hear a description of the catastrophe from the buffoon under the table, and platitudinously to moralize that the perfidious wretch, having been stored away safely in the realm of Pluto and Proserpine, nothing remained for them to do except to raise their voices in the words of the "old song,"

"Questo ?il fin di chi fa mal: E dei perfidi la morte Alla vita ?sempre ugual."

"New York Musical Season, 1889-90."

[F] "Review of the New York Musical Season, 1889-90," p. 75.

[G] See "Studies in the Wagnerian Drama," chapter I.

VIII

Choirs and Choral Music

[Sidenote: Choirs a touchstone of culture.]

[Sidenote: The value of choir singing.]

No one would go far astray who should estimate the extent and sincerity of a community's musical culture by the number of its chorus singers. Some years ago it was said that over three hundred cities and towns in Germany contained singing societies and orchestras devoted to the cultivation of choral music. In the United States, where there are comparatively a small number of instrumental musicians, there has been a wonderful development of singing societies within the last generation, and it is to this fact largely that the notable growth in the country's knowledge and appreciation of high-class music is due. No amount of mere hearing and study can compare in influence with participation in musical performance. Music is an art which rests on love. It is beautiful sound vitalized by feeling, and it can only be grasped fully through man's emotional nature. There is no quicker or surer way to get to the heart of a composition than by performing it, and since participation in chorus singing is of necessity unselfish and creative of sympathy, there is no better medium of musical culture than membership in a choir. It was because he realized this that Schumann gave the advice to all students of music: "Sing diligently in choirs; especially the middle voices, for this will make you musical."

[Sidenote: Singing societies and orchestras.]

[Sidenote: Neither numbers nor wealth necessary.]

There is no community so small or so ill-conditioned that it cannot maintain a singing society. Before a city can give sustenance to even a small body of instrumentalists it must be large enough and rich enough to maintain a theatre from which those instrumentalists can derive their support. There can be no dependence upon amateurs, for people do not study the oboe, bassoon, trombone, or double-bass for amusement. Amateur violinists and amateur flautists there are in plenty, but not amateur clarinetists and French-horn players; but if the love for music exists in a community, a dozen families shall suffice to maintain a choral club. Large numbers are therefore not essential; neither is wealth. Some of the largest and finest choirs in the world flourish among the Welsh miners in the United States and Wales, fostered by a native love for the art and the national institution called Eisteddfod.

[Sidenote: Lines of choral culture in the United States.]

The lines on which choral culture has proceeded in the United States are two, of which the more valuable, from an artistic point of view, is that of the oratorio, which went out from New England. The other originated in the German cultivation of the Menergesang, the importance of which is felt more in the extent of the culture, prompted as it is largely by social considerations, than in the music sung, which is of necessity of a lower grade than that composed for mixed voices. It is chiefly in the impulse which German Menergesang carried into all the corners of the land, and especially the impetus which the festivals of the German singers gave to the sections in which they have been held for half a century, that this form of culture is interesting.

[Sidenote: Church and oratorio.]

[Sidenote: Secular choirs.]

The cultivation of oratorio music sprang naturally from the Church, and though it is now chiefly in the hands of secular societies, the biblical origin of the vast majority of the texts used in the works which are performed, and more especially the regular performances of Handel's "Messiah" in the Christmastide, have left the notion, more or less distinct, in the public mind, that oratorios are religious functions. Nevertheless (or perhaps because of this fact) the most successful choral concerts in the United States are those given by oratorio societies. The cultivation of choral music which is secular in character is chiefly in the hands of small organizations, whose concerts are of a semi-private nature and are enjoyed by the associate members and invited guests. This circumstance is deserving of notice as a characteristic feature of choral music in America, though it has no particular bearing upon this study, which must concern itself with choral organizations, choral music, and choral performances in general.

[Sidenote: Amateur choirs originated in the United States.]

[Sidenote: The size of old choirs.]

Organizations of the kind in view differ from instrumental in being composed of amateurs; and amateur choir-singing is no older anywhere than in the United States. Two centuries ago and more the singing of catches and glees was a common amusement among the gentler classes in England, but the performances of the larger forms of choral music were in the hands of professional choristers who were connected with churches, theatres, schools, and other public institutions. Naturally, then, the choral bodies were small. Choirs of hundreds and thousands, such as take part in the festivals of to-day, are a product of a later time.

[Sidenote: Handel's choirs.]

"When Bach and Handel wrote their Passions, Church Cantatas, and Oratorios, they could only dream of such majestic performances as those works receive now; and it is one of the miracles of art that they should have written in so masterly a manner for forces that they could never hope to control. Who would think, when listening to the 'Hallelujah' of 'The Messiah,' or the great double choruses of 'Israel in Egypt,' in which the voice of the composer is 'as the voice of a great multitude, and as the voice of many waters, and as the voice of many thunderings, saying, "Alleluia, for the Lord God Omnipotent reigneth!"' that these colossal compositions were never heard by Handel from any chorus larger than the most modest of our church choirs? At the last performance of 'The Messiah' at which Handel was advertised to appear (it was for the benefit of his favorite charity, the Foundling Hospital, on May 3, 1759--he died before the time, however), the singers, including principals, numbered twenty-three, while the instrumentalists numbered thirty-three. At the first great Handel Commemoration, in Westminster Abbey, in 1784, the choir numbered two hundred and seventy-five, the band two hundred and fifty; and this was the most numerous force ever gathered together for a single performance in England up to that time.

[Sidenote: Choirs a century ago.]

[Sidenote: Bach's choir.]

"In 1791 the Commemoration was celebrated by a choir of five hundred and a band of three hundred and seventy-five. In May, 1786, Johann Adam Hiller, one of Bach's successors as cantor of the St. Thomas School in Leipsic, directed what was termed a Massenauff 薫 rung of 'The Messiah,' in the Domkirche, in Berlin. His 'masses' consisted of one hundred and eighteen singers and one hundred and eighty-six instrumentalists. In Handel's operas, and sometimes even in his oratorios, the tutti meant, in his time, little more than a union of all the solo singers; and even Bach's Passion music and church cantatas, which seem as much designed for numbers as the double choruses of 'Israel,' were rendered in the St. Thomas Church by a ludicrously small choir. Of this fact a record is preserved in the archives of Leipsic. In August, 1730, Bach submitted to the authorities a plan for a church choir of the pupils in his care. In this plan his singers numbered twelve, there being one principal and two ripienists in each voice; with characteristic modesty he barely suggests a preference for sixteen. The circumstance that in the same document he asked for at least eighteen instrumentalists (two more if flutes were used), taken in connection with the figures given relative to the 'Messiah' performances, gives an insight into the relations between the vocal and the instrumental parts of a choral performance in those days."[H]

[Sidenote: Proportion of voices and instruments.]

This relation has been more than reversed since then, the orchestras at modern oratorio performances seldom being one-fifth as large as the choir. This difference, however, is due largely to the changed character of modern music, that of to-day treating the instruments as independent agents of expression instead of using them chiefly to support the voices and add sonority to the tonal mass, as was done by Handel and most of the composers of his day.

[Sidenote: Glee unions and male choirs.]

I omit from consideration the Glee Unions of England, and the quartets, which correspond to them, in this country. They are not cultivators of choral music, and the music which they sing is an insignificant factor in culture. The male choirs, too, need not detain us long, since it may be said without injustice that their mission is more social than artistic. In these choirs the subdivision into parts is, as a rule, into two tenor voices, first and second, and two bass, first and second. In the glee unions, the effect of whose singing is fairly well imitated by the college clubs of the United States (pitiful things, indeed, from an artistic point of view), there is a survival of an old element in the male alto singing above the melody voice, generally in a painful falsetto. This abomination is unknown to the German part-songs for men's voices, which are written normally, but are in the long run monotonous in color for want of the variety in timbre and register which the female voices contribute in a mixed choir.

[Sidenote: Women's choirs.]

There are choirs also composed exclusively of women, but they are even more unsatisfactory than the male choirs, for the reason that the absence of the bass voice leaves their harmony without sufficient foundation. Generally, music for these choirs is written for three parts, two sopranos and contralto, with the result that it hovers, suspended like Mahomet's coffin, between heaven and earth. When a fourth part is added it is a second contralto, which is generally carried down to the tones that are hollow and unnatural.

[Sidenote: Boys' choirs.]

The substitution of boys for women in Episcopal Church choirs has grown extensively within the last ten years in the United States, very much to the promotion of aesthetic sentimentality in the congregations, but without improving the character of worship-music. Boys' voices are practically limitless in an upward direction, and are naturally clear and penetrating. Ravishing effects can be produced with them, but it is false art to use passionless voices in music conceived for the mature and emotional voices of adults; and very little of the old English Cathedral music, written for choirs of boys and men, is preserved in the service lists to-day.

[Sidenote: Mixed choirs.]

The only satisfactory choirs are the mixed choirs of men and women. Upon them has devolved the cultivation of artistic choral music in our public concert-rooms. As we know such choirs now, they are of comparatively recent origin, and it is a singular commentary upon the way in which musical history is written, that the fact should have so long been overlooked that the credit of organizing the first belongs to the United States. A little reflection will show this fact, which seems somewhat startling at first blush, to be entirely natural. Large singing societies are of necessity made up of amateurs, and the want of professional musicians in America compelled the people to enlist amateurs at a time when in Europe choral activity rested on the church, theatre, and institute choristers, who were practically professionals.

[Sidenote: Origin of amateur singing societies.]

[Sidenote: The German record.]

[Sidenote: American priority.]

[Sidenote: The American record.]

As the hitherto accepted record stands, the first amateur singing society was the Singakademie of Berlin, which Carl Friedrich Fasch, accompanist to the royal flautist, Frederick the Great, called into existence in 1791. A few dates will show how slow the other cities of musical Germany were in following Berlin's example. In 1818 there were only ten amateur choirs in all Germany. Leipsic organized one in 1800, Stettin in 1800, Munster in 1804, Dresden in 1807, Potsdam in 1814, Bremen in 1815, Chemnitz in 1817, Schwisch-Hall in 1817, and Innsbruck in 1818. The Berlin Singakademie is still in existence, but so also is the Stoughton Musical Society in Stoughton, Mass., which was founded on November 7, 1786. Mr. Charles C. Perkins, historian of the Handel and Haydn Society, whose foundation was coincident with the sixth society in Germany (Bremen, 1815), enumerates the following predecessors of that venerable organization: the Stoughton Musical Society, 1786; Independent Musical Society, "established at Boston in the same year, which gave a concert at King's Chapel in 1788, and took part there in commemorating the death of Washington (December 14, 1799) on his first succeeding birthday;" the Franklin, 1804; the Salem, 1806; Massachusetts Musical, 1807; Lock Hospital, 1812, and the Norfolk Musical, the date of whose foundation is not given by Mr. Perkins.

[Sidenote: Choirs in the West.]

When the Bremen Singakademie was organized there were already choirs in the United States as far west as Cincinnati. In that city they were merely church choirs at first, but within a few years they had combined into a large body and were giving concerts at which some of the choruses of Handel and Haydn were sung. That their performances, as well as those of the New England societies, were cruder than those of their European rivals may well be believed, but with this I have nothing to do. I am simply seeking to establish the priority of the United States in amateur choral culture. The number of American cities in which oratorios are performed annually is now about fifty.

[Sidenote: The size of choirs.]

[Sidenote: Large numbers not essential.]

[Sidenote: How "divisions" used to be sung.]

In size mixed choirs ordinarily range from forty voices to five hundred. It were well if it were understood by choristers as well as the public that numbers merely are not a sign of merit in a singing society. So the concert-room be not too large, a choir of sixty well-trained voices is large enough to perform almost everything in choral literature with good effect, and the majority of the best compositions will sound better under such circumstances than in large rooms with large choirs. Especially is this true of the music of the Middle Ages, written for voices without instrumental accompaniment, of which I shall have something to say when the discussion reaches choral programmes. There is music, it is true, like much of Handel's, the impressiveness of which is greatly enhanced by masses, but it is not extensive enough to justify the sacrifice of correctness and finish in the performance to mere volume. The use of large choirs has had the effect of developing the skilfulness of amateur singers in an astonishing degree, but there is, nevertheless, a point where weightiness of tone becomes an obstacle to finished execution. When Mozart remodelled Handel's "Messiah" he was careful to indicate that the florid passages ("divisions" they used to be called in England) should be sung by the solo voices alone, but nowadays choirs of five hundred voices attack such choruses as "For unto us a Child is Born," without the slightest hesitation, even if they sometimes make a mournful mess of the "divisions."

[Sidenote: The division of choirs.]

[Sidenote: Five-part music.]

[Sidenote: Eight part.]

[Sidenote: Antiphonal music.]

[Sidenote: Bach's "St. Matthew Passion."]

The normal division of a mixed choir is into four parts or voices--soprano, contralto, tenor, and bass; but composers sometimes write for more parts, and the choir is subdivided to correspond. The custom of writing for five, six, eight, ten, and even more voices was more common in the Middle Ages, the palmy days of the a capella (i.e., for the chapel, unaccompanied) style than it is now, and, as a rule, a division into more than four voices is not needed outside of the societies which cultivate this old music, such as the Musical Art Society in New York, the Bach Choir in London, and the Domchor in Berlin. In music for five parts, one of the upper voices, soprano or tenor, is generally doubled; for six, the ordinary distribution is into two sopranos, two contraltos, tenor, and bass. When eight voices are reached a distinction is made according as there are to be eight real parts (a otto voci reali), or two choruses of the four normal parts each (a otto voci in due cori reali). In the first instance the arrangement commonly is three sopranos, two contraltos, two tenors, and one bass. One of the most beautiful uses of the double choir is to produce antiphonal effects, choir answering to choir, both occasionally uniting in the climaxes. How stirring this effect can be made may be observed in some of Bach's compositions, especially those in which he makes the division of the choir subserve a dramatic purpose, as in the first chorus of "The Passion according to St. Matthew," where the two choirs, one representing Daughters of Zion, the other Believers, interrogate and answer each other thus:

I. "Come, ye daughters, weep for anguish; See Him! II. "Whom? I. "The Son of Man. See Him! II. "How? I. "So like a lamb. See it! II. "What? I. "His love untold. Look! II. "Look where? I. "Our guilt behold."

[Sidenote: Antiphony in a motet.]

Another most striking instance is in the same master's motet, "Sing ye to the Lord," which is written for two choirs of four parts each. (In the example from the "St. Matthew Passion" there is a third choir of soprano voices which sings a chorale while the dramatic choirs are conversing.) In the motet the first choir begins a fugue, in the midst of which the second choir is heard shouting jubilantly, "Sing ye! Sing ye! Sing ye!" Then the choirs change roles, the first delivering the injunction, the second singing the fugue. In modern music, composers frequently consort a quartet of solo voices, soprano, contralto, tenor, and bass, with a four-part chorus, and thus achieve fine effects of contrast in dynamics and color, as well as antiphonal.

[Sidenote: Excellence in choral singing.]

[Sidenote: Community of action.]

[Sidenote: Individualism.]

[Sidenote: Dynamics.]

[Sidenote: Beauty of tone.]

[Sidenote: Contralto voices.]

The question is near: What constitutes excellence in a choral performance? To answer: The same qualities that constitute excellence in an orchestral performance, will scarcely suffice, except as a generalization. A higher degree of harmonious action is exacted of a body of singers than of a body of instrumentalists. Many of the parts in a symphony are played by a single instrument. Community of voice belongs only to each of the five bodies of string-players. In a chorus there are from twelve to one hundred and fifty voices, or even more, united in each part. This demands the effacement of individuality in a chorus, upon the assertion of which, in a band, under the judicious guidance of the conductor, many of the effects of color and expression depend. Each group in a choir must strive for homogeneity of voice quality; each singer must sink the ego in the aggregation, yet employ it in its highest potency so far as the mastery of the technics of singing is concerned. In cultivating precision of attack (i.e., promptness in beginning a tone and leaving it off), purity of intonation (i.e., accuracy or justness of pitch--"singing in tune" according to the popular phrase), clearness of enunciation, and careful attention to all the dynamic gradations of tone, from very soft up to very loud, and all shades of expression between, in the development of that gradual augmentation of tone called crescendo, and the gradual diminution called diminuendo, the highest order of individual skill is exacted from every chorister; for upon individual perfection in these things depends the collective effect which it is the purpose of the conductor to achieve. Sensuous beauty of tone, even in large aggregations, is also dependent to a great degree upon careful and proper emission of voice by each individual, and it is because the contralto part in most choral music, being a middle part, lies so easily in the voices of the singers that the contralto contingent in American choirs, especially, so often attracts attention by the charm of its tone. Contralto voices are seldom forced into the regions which compel so great a physical strain that beauty and character must be sacrificed to mere accomplishment of utterance, as is frequently the case with the soprano part.

[Sidenote: Selfishness fatal to success.]

[Sidenote: Tonal balance.]

Yet back of all this exercise of individual skill there must be a spirit of self-sacrifice which can only exist in effective potency if prompted by universal sympathy and love for the art. A selfish chorister is not a chorister, though possessed of the voice of a Melba or Mario. Balance between the parts, not only in the fundamental constitution of the choir but also in all stages of a performance, is also a matter of the highest consideration. In urban communities, especially, it is difficult to secure perfect tonal symmetry--the rule is a poverty in tenor voices--but those who go to hear choral concerts are entitled to hear a well-balanced choir, and the presence of an army of sopranos will not condone a squad of tenors. Again, I say, better a well-balanced small choir than an ill-balanced large one.

[Sidenote: Declamation.]

[Sidenote: Expression.]

[Sidenote: The choruses in "The Messiah."]

[Sidenote: Variety of declamation in Handel's oratorio.]

I have not enumerated all the elements which enter into a meritorious performance, nor shall I discuss them all; only in passing do I wish to direct attention to one which shines by its absence in the choral performances not only of America but also of Great Britain and Germany. Proper pronunciation of the texts is an obvious requirement; so ought also to be declamation. There is no reason why characteristic expression, by which I mean expression which goes to the genius of the melodic phrase when it springs from the verbal, should be ignored, simply because it may be difficult of attainment from large bodies of singers. There is so much monotony in oratorio concerts because all oratorios and all parts of any single oratorio are sung alike. Only when the "Hallelujah" is sung in "The Messiah" at the gracious Christmastide is an exaltation above the dull level of the routine performances noticeable, and then it is communicated to the singers by the act of the listeners in rising to their feet. Now, despite the structural sameness in the choruses of "The Messiah," they have a great variety of content, and if the characteristic physiognomy of each could but be disclosed, the grand old work, which seems hackneyed to so many, would acquire amazing freshness, eloquence, and power. Then should we be privileged to note that there is ample variety in the voice of the old master, of whom a greater than he said that when he wished, he could strike like a thunderbolt. Then should we hear the tones of amazed adoration in

[Music illustration: Be-hold the Lamb of God!]

of cruel scorn in

[Music illustration: He trust-ed in God that would de-li-ver Him, let him de-li-ver him if he de-light in him.]

of boastfulness and conscious strength in

[Music illustration: Let us break their bonds a-sun-der.]

and learn to admire as we ought to admire the declamatory strength and truthfulness so common in Handel's choruses.

[Sidenote: Medieval music.]

[Sidenote: Madrigals.]

There is very little cultivation of choral music of the early ecclesiastical type, and that little is limited to the Church and a few choirs specially organized for its performance, like those that I have mentioned. This music is so foreign to the conceptions of the ordinary amateur, and exacts so much skill in the singing of the intervals, lacking the prop of modern tonality as it does, that it is seldom that an amateur body can be found equal to its performance. Moreover, it is nearly all of a solemn type. Its composers were churchmen, and when it was written nearly all that there was of artistic music was in the service of the Church. The secular music of the time consisted chiefly in Madrigals, which differed from ecclesiastical music only in their texts, they being generally erotic in sentiment. The choristers of to-day, no less than the public, find it difficult to appreciate them, because they are not melodic in the sense that most music is nowadays. In them the melody is not the privileged possession of the soprano voice. All the voices stand on an equal footing, and the composition consists of a weaving together, according to scientific rules, of a number of voices--counterpoint as it is called.

[Sidenote: Homophonic hymns.]

[Sidenote: Calvin's restrictive influence.]

Our hymn-tunes are homophonic, based upon a melody sung by one voice, for which the other voices provide the harmony. This style of music came into the Church through the German Reformation. Though Calvin was a lover of music he restricted its practice among his followers to unisonal psalmody, that is, to certain tunes adapted to the versified psalms sung without accompaniment of harmony voices. On the adoption of the Genevan psalter he gave the strictest injunction that neither its text nor its melodies were to be altered.

"Those songs and melodies," said he, "which are composed for the mere pleasure of the ear, and all they call ornamental music, and songs for four parts, do not behoove the majesty of the Church, and cannot fail greatly to displease God."

[Sidenote: Luther and the German Church.]

Under the influence of the German reformers music was in a very different case. Luther was not only an amateur musician, he was also an ardent lover of scientific music. Josquin des Pres, a contemporary of Columbus, was his greatest admiration; nevertheless, he was anxious from the beginning of his work of Church establishment to have the music of the German Church German in spirit and style. In 1525 he wrote:

[Sidenote: A German mass.]

"I should like to have a German mass, and I am indeed at work on one; but I am anxious that it shall be truly German in manner. I have no objection to a translated Latin text and Latin notes; but they are neither proper nor just (_aber es lautet nicht artig noch rechtschaffen_); text and notes, accent, melodies, and demeanor must come from our mother tongue and voice, else will it all be but a mimicry, like that of the apes."

[Sidenote: Secular tunes used.]

[Sidenote: Congregational singing.]

In the Church music of the time, composed, as I have described, by a scientific interweaving of voices, the composers had got into the habit of utilizing secular melodies as the foundation on which to build their contrapuntal structures. I have no doubt that it was the spirit which speaks out of Luther's words which brought it to pass that in Germany contrapuntal music with popular melodies as foundations developed into the chorale, in which the melody and not the counterpoint was the essential thing. With the Lutheran Church came congregational singing; with congregational singing the need of a new style of composition, which should not only make the participation of the people in the singing possible, but should also stimulate them to sing by freeing the familiar melodies (the melodies of folk-songs) from the elaborate and ingenious, but soulless, counterpoint which fettered them.

[Sidenote: Counterpoint.]

[Sidenote: The first congregational hymns.]

The Flemish masters, who were the musical law-givers, had been using secular tunes for over a century, but only as stalking-horses for counterpoint; and when the Germans began to use their tunes, they, too, buried them beyond recognition in the contrapuntal mass. The people were invited to sing paraphrases of the psalms to familiar tunes, it is true, but the choir's polyphony went far to stifle the spirit of the melody. Soon the free spirit which I have repeatedly referred to as Romanticism, and which was powerfully encouraged by the Reformation, prompted a style of composition in which the admired melody was lifted into relief. This could not be done until the new style of writing invented by the creators of the opera (see Chapter VII.) came in, but as early as 1568 Dr. Lucas Ostrander published fifty hymns and psalms with music so arranged "that the congregation may join in singing them." This, then, is in outline the story of the beginning of modern hymnology, and it is recalled to the patrons of choral concerts whenever in

Bach's "Passion Music" or in Mendelssohn's "St. Paul" the choir sings one of the marvellous old hymns of the German Church.

[Sidenote: The Church and conservatism.]

[Sidenote: Harmony and emotion.]

Choral music being bound up with the Church, it has naturally participated in the conservatism characteristic of the Church. The severe old style has survived in the choral compositions of to-day, while instrumental music has grown to be almost a new thing within the century which is just closing. It is the severe style established by Bach, however, not that of Palestrina. In the Church compositions prior to Palestrina the emotional power of harmony was but little understood. The harmonies, indeed, were the accidents of the interweaving of melodies. Palestrina was among the first to feel the uplifting effect which might result from a simple sequence of pure consonant harmonies, and the three chords which open his famous "Stabat Mater"

[Sidenote: Palestrina's "Stabat Mater."]

[Sidenote: Characteristics of his music.]

[Music illustration: Sta-bat ma-ter]

are a sign of his style as distinct in its way as the devices by means of which Wagner stamps his individuality on his phrases. His melodies, too, compared with the artificial motivi of his predecessors, are distinguished by grace, beauty, and expressiveness, while his command of æ herial effects, due to the manner in which the voices are combined, is absolutely without parallel from his day to this. Of the mystery of pure beauty he enjoyed a wonderful revelation, and has handed it down to us in such works as the "Stabat Mater," "Missa Pap?Marcelli," and the "Improperia."

[Sidenote: Palestrina's music not dramatic.]

[Sidenote: A churchman.]

[Sidenote: Effect of the Reformation.]

This music must not be listened to with the notion in mind of dramatic expression such as we almost instinctively feel to-day. Palestrina does not seek to proclaim the varying sentiment which underlies his texts. That leads to individual interpretation and is foreign to the habits of churchmen in the old conception, when the individual was completely resolved in the organization. He aimed to exalt the mystery of the service, not to bring it down to popular comprehension and make it a personal utterance. For such a design in music we must wait until after the Reformation, when the ancient mysticism began to fall back before the demands of reason, when the idea of the sole and sufficient mediation of the Church lost some of its power in the face of the growing conviction of intimate personal relationship between man and his creator. Now idealism had to yield some of its dominion to realism, and a more rugged art grew up in place of that which had been so wonderfully sublimated by mysticism.

[Sidenote: The source of beauty in Palestrina's music.]

It is in Bach, who came a century after Palestrina, that we find the most eloquent musical proclamation of the new regime, and it is in no sense disrespectful to the great German master if we feel that the change in ideals was accompanied with a loss in sensuous charm, or pure aesthetic beauty. Effect has had to yield to idea. It is in the flow of the voices, the color effects which result from combination and registers, the clarity of the harmonies, the reposefulness coming from conscious ease of utterance, the loveliness of each individual part, and the spiritual exaltation of the whole that the aesthetic mystery of Palestrina's music lies.

[Sidenote: Bach.]

Like Palestrina, Bach is the culmination of the musical practice of his time, but, unlike Palestrina, he is also the starting-point of a new development. With Bach the old contrapuntal art, now not vocal merely but instrumental also and mixed, reaches its climax, and the tendency sets in which leads to the highly complex and dramatic art of to-day. Palestrina's art is Roman; the spirit of restfulness, of celestial calm, of supernatural revelation and supernal beauty broods over it. Bach's is Gothic--rugged, massive, upward striving, human. In Palestrina's music the voice that speaks is the voice of angels; in

Bach's it is the voice of men.

[Sidenote: Bach a German Protestant.]

[Sidenote: Church and individual.]

[Sidenote: Ingenuousness of feeling.]

Bach is the publisher of the truest, tenderest, deepest, and most individual religious feeling. His music is peculiarly a hymning of the religious sentiment of Protestant Germany, where salvation is to be wrought out with fear and trembling by each individual through faith and works rather than the agency of even a divinely constituted Church. It reflects, with rare fidelity and clearness, the essential qualities of the German people--their warm sympathy, profound compassion, fervent love, and sturdy faith. As the Church fell into the background and the individual came to the fore, religious music took on the dramatic character which we find in the "Passion Music" of Bach. Here the sufferings and death of the Saviour, none the less an ineffable mystery, are depicted as the most poignant experience of each individual believer, and with an ingenuousness that must forever provoke the wonder of those who are unable to enter into the German nature. The worshippers do not hesitate to say: "My Jesus, good-night!" as they gather in fancy around His tomb and invoke sweet rest for His weary limbs. The difference between such a proclamation and the calm voice of the Church should be borne in mind when comparing the music of Palestrina with that of Bach; also the vast strides made by music during the intervening century.

[Sidenote: The motet.]

Of Bach's music we have in the repertories of our best choral societies a number of motets, church cantatas, a setting of the "Magnificat," and the great mass in B minor. The term Motet lacks somewhat of definiteness of the usage of composers. Originally it seems likely that it was a secular composition which the Netherland composers enlisted in the service of the Church by adapting it to Biblical and other religious texts. Then it was always unaccompanied. In the later Protestant motets the chorale came to play a great part; the various stanzas of a hymn were given different settings, the foundation of each being the hymn tune. These were interspersed with independent pieces, based on Biblical words.

[Sidenote: Church cantatas.]

The Church Cantatas (Kirchencantaten) are larger services with orchestral accompaniment, which were written to conform to the various religious festivals and Sundays of the year; each has for a fundamental subject the theme which is proper to the day. Again, a chorale provides the musical foundation. Words and melody are retained, but between the stanzas occur recitatives and metrical airs, or ariosos, for solo voices in the nature of commentaries or reflections on the sentiment of the hymn or the gospel lesson for the day.

[Sidenote: The "Passions."]

[Sidenote: Origin of the "Passions."]

[Sidenote: Early Holy Week services.]

The "Passions" are still more extended, and were written for use in the Reformed Church in Holy Week. As an art-form they are unique, combining a number of elements and having all the apparatus of an oratorio plus the congregation, which took part in the performance by singing the hymns dispersed through the work. The service (for as a service, rather than as an oratorio, it must be treated) roots in the Miracle plays and Mysteries of the Middle Ages, but its origin is even more remote, going back to the custom followed by the primitive Christians of making the reading of the story of the Passion a special service for Holy Week. In the Eastern Church it was introduced in a simple dramatic form as early as the fourth century A.D., the treatment being somewhat like the ancient tragedies, the text being intoned or chanted. In the Western Church, until the sixteenth century, the Passion was read in a way which gave the service one element which is found in Bach's works in an amplified form. Three deacons were employed, one to read (or rather chant to Gregorian melodies) the words of Christ, another to deliver the narrative in the words of the Evangelist, and a third to give the utterances and exclamations of the Apostles and people. This was the _Cantus Passionis Domini nostri Jesu Christe_ of the Church, and had so strong a hold upon the tastes of the people that it was preserved by Luther in the Reformed Church.

[Sidenote: The service amplified.]

[Sidenote: Bach's settings.]

Under this influence it was speedily amplified. The successive steps of the progress are not clear, but the choir seems to have first succeeded to the part formerly sung by the third deacon, and in some churches the whole Passion was sung antiphonally by two choirs. In the seventeenth century the introduction of recitatives and arias, distributed among singers who represented the personages of sacred history, increased the dramatic element of the service which reached its climax in the "St. Matthew" setting by Bach. The chorales are supposed to have been introduced about 1704. Bach's "Passions" are the last that figure in musical history. That "according to St. John" is performed occasionally in Germany, but it yields the palm of excellence to that "according to St. Matthew," which had its first performance on Good Friday, 1729, in Leipsic. It is in two parts, which were formerly separated by the sermon, and employs two choirs, each with its own orchestra, solo singers in all the classes of voices, and a harpsichord to accompany all the recitatives, except those of Jesus, which are distinguished by being accompanied by the orchestral strings.

[Sidenote: Oratorios.]

[Sidenote: Sacred operas.]

In the nature of things passions, oratorios, and their secular cousins, cantatas, imply scenes and actions, and therefore have a remote kinship with the lyric drama. The literary analogy which they suggest is the epic poem as contra-distinguished from the drama. While the drama presents incident, the oratorio relates, expounds, and celebrates, presenting it to the fancy through the ear instead of representing it to the eye. A great deal of looseness has crept into this department of music as into every other, and the various forms have been approaching each other until in some cases it is become difficult to say which term, opera or oratorio, ought to be applied. Rubinstein's "sacred operas" are oratorios profusely interspersed with stage directions, many of which are impossible of scenic realization. Their whole purpose is to work upon the imagination of the listeners and thus open gate-ways for the music. Ever since its composition, Saint-Saëns's "Samson and Delilah" has held a place in both theatre and concert-room. Liszt's "St. Elizabeth" has been found more effective when provided with pictorial accessories than without. The greater part of "Elijah" might be presented in dramatic form.

[Sidenote: Influence of the Church plays.]

[Sidenote: Origin of the oratorio.]

[Sidenote: The choral element extended.]

[Sidenote: Narrative and descriptive choruses.]

[Sidenote: Dramatization.]

Confusing and anomalous as these things are, they find their explanation in the circumstance that the oratorio never quite freed itself from the influence of the people's Church plays in which it had its beginning. As a distinct art-form it began in a mixture of artistic entertainment and religious worship provided in the early part of the sixteenth century by Filippo Neri (now a saint) for those who came for pious instruction to his oratory (whence the name). The purpose of these entertainments being religious, the subjects were Biblical, and though the musical progress from the beginning was along the line of the lyric drama, contemporaneous in origin with it, the music naturally developed into broader forms on the choral side, because music had to make up for the lack of pantomime, costumes, and scenery. Hence we have not only the preponderance of choruses in the oratorio over recitative, arias, duets, trios, and so forth, but also the adherence in the choral part to the old manner of writing which made the expansion of the choruses possible. Where the choruses left the field of pure reflection and became narrative, as in "Israel in Egypt," or assumed a dramatic character, as in the "Elijah," the composer found in them vehicles for descriptive and characteristic music, and so local color came into use. Characterization of the solo parts followed as a matter of course, an early illustration being found in the manner in which Bach lifted the words of Christ into prominence by surrounding them with the radiant halo which streams from the violin accompaniment. In consequence the singer to whom was assigned the task of singing the part of Jesus presented himself to the fancy of the listeners as a representative of the historical personage--as the Christ of the drama.

[Sidenote: The chorus in opera and oratorio.]

The growth of the instrumental art here came admirably into play, and so it came to pass that opera and oratorio now have their musical elements of expression in common, and differ only in their application of them--opera foregoing the choral element to a great extent as being a hindrance to action, and oratorio elevating it to make good the absence of scenery and action. While oratorios are biblical and legendary, cantatas deal with secular subjects and, in the form of dramatic ballads, find a delightful field in the world of romance and supernaturalism.

[Sidenote: The Mass.]

[Sidenote: Secularization of the Mass.]

Transferred from the Church to the concert-room, and considered as an art-form instead of the eucharistic office, the Mass has always made a strong appeal to composers, and half a dozen masterpieces of missal composition hold places in the concert lists of the singing societies. Notable among these are the Requiems of Mozart, Berlioz, and Verdi, and the Solemn Mass in D by Beethoven. These works represent at one and the same time the climax of accomplishment in the musical treatment and the secularization of the missal text. They are the natural outcome of the expansion of the office by the introduction of the orchestra into the Church, the departure from the a capella style of writing, which could not be consorted with the orchestra, and the growth of a desire to enhance the pomp of great occasions in the Church by the production of masses specially composed for them. Under such circumstances the devotional purpose of the mass was lost in the artistic, and composers gave free reign to their powers, for which they found an ample stimulus in the missal text.

[Sidenote: Sentimental masses.]

[Sidenote: Mozart and the Mass.]

[Sidenote: The masses for the dead.]

[Sidenote: Gossec's Requiem.]

The first effect, and the one which largely justifies the adherents of the old ecclesiastical style in their crusade against the Catholic Church music of to-day, was to make the masses sentimental and operatic. So little regard was had for the sentiment of the words, so little respect for the solemnity of the sacrament, that more than a century ago Mozart (whose masses are far from being models of religious expression) could say to Cantor Doles of a Gloria which the latter showed him, "S'ist ja alles nix," and immediately sing the music to "Hol's der Geier, das geht flink!" which words, he said, went better. The liberty begotten by this license, though it tended to ruin the mass, considered strictly as a liturgical service, developed it musically. The masses for the dead were among the earliest to feel the spirit of the time, for in the sequence, Dies iris, they contained the dramatic element which the solemn mass lacked. The Kyrie, Credo, Gloria, Sanctus, and Agnus Dei are purely lyrical, and though the evolutionary movement ended in Beethoven conceiving certain portions (notably the Agnus Dei) in a dramatic sense, it was but natural that so far as tradition fixed the disposition and formal style of the various parts, it should not be disturbed. At an early date the composers began to put forth their powers of description in the Dies ir? however, and there is extant in a French mass an amusing example of the length to which tone-painting in this music was carried by them. Gossec wrote a Requiem on the death of Mirabeau which became famous. The words, Quantus tremor est futurus, he set so that on each syllable there were repetitions, staccato, of a single tone, thus:

This absurd stuttering Gossec designed to picture the terror inspired by the coming of the Judge at the last trumpet.

[Sidenote: The orchestra in the Mass.]

[Sidenote: Beethoven and Berlioz.]

The development of instrumentation placed a factor in the hands of these writers which they were not slow to utilize, especially in writing music for the Dies ir? and how effectively Mozart used the orchestra in his Requiem it is not necessary to state. It is a safe assumption that Beethoven's Mass in D was largely instrumental in inspiring Berlioz to set the Requiem as he did. With Beethoven the dramatic idea is the controlling one, and so it is with Berlioz. Beethoven, while showing a reverence for the formulas of the Church, and respecting the tradition which gave the Kyrie a triple division and made fugue movements out of the phrases "_Cum sancto spiritu in gloria Dei patris--Amen," "Et vitam venturi," and "Osanna in excelsis_," nevertheless gave his composition a scope which placed it beyond the apparatus of the Church, and filled it with a spirit that spurns the limitations of any creed of less breadth and universality than the grand Theism which affectionate communion with nature had taught him.

[Sidenote: Berlioz's Requiem.]

[Sidenote: Dramatic effects in Haydn's masses.]

[Sidenote: Berlioz's orchestra.]

Berlioz, less religious, less reverential, but equally fired by the solemnity and majesty of the matter given into his hands, wrote a work in which he placed his highest conception of the awfulness of the Last Judgment and the emotions which are awakened by its contemplation. In respect of the instrumentation he showed a far greater audacity than Beethoven displayed even in the much-mooted trumpets and drums of the Agnus Dei, where he introduces the sounds of war to heighten the intensity of the prayer for peace, "_Dona nobis pacem_." This is talked about in the books as a bold innovation. It seems to have escaped notice that the idea had occurred to Haydn twenty-four years before and been realized by him. In 1796 Haydn wrote a mass, "In Tempore Belli," the French army being at the time in Steyermark. He set the words, "Agnus Dei qui tollis peccata mundi," to an accompaniment of drums, "as if the enemy were already heard coming in the distance." He went farther than this in a Mass in D minor, when he accompanied the Benedictus with fanfares of trumpets. But all such timid ventures in the use of instruments in the mass sink into utter insignificance when compared with Berlioz's apparatus in the Tuba mirum of his Requiem, which supplements the ordinary symphonic orchestra, some of its instruments already doubled, with four brass bands of eight or ten instruments each, sixteen extra drums, and a tam-tam.

FOOTNOTES:

[H] "Notes on the Cultivation of Choral Music," by H.E. Krehbiel, p. 17.

IX

Musician, Critic, and Public

[Sidenote: The newspapers and the public.]

I have been told that there are many people who read the newspapers on the day after they have attended a concert or operatic representation for the purpose of finding out whether or not the performance gave them proper or sufficient enjoyment. It would not be becoming in me to inquire too curiously into the truth of such a statement, and in view of a denunciation spoken in the introductory chapter of this book, I am not sure that it is not a piece of arrogance, or impudence, on my part to undertake in any way to justify any critical writing on the subject of music. Certain it is that some men who write about music for the newspapers believe, or affect to believe, that criticism is worthless, and I shall not escape the charge of inconsistency, if, after I have condemned the blunders of literary men, who are laymen in music, and separated the majority of professional writers on the art into pedants and rhapsodists, I nevertheless venture to discuss the nature and value of musical criticism. Yet, surely, there must be a right and wrong in this as in every other thing, and just as surely the present structure of society, which rests on the newspaper, invites attention to the existing relationship between musician, critic, and public as an important element in the question How to Listen to Music.

[Sidenote: Relationship between musician, critic, and public.]

[Sidenote: The need and value of conflict.]

As a condition precedent to the discussion of this new element in the case, I lay down the proposition that the relationship between the three factors enumerated is so intimate and so strict that the world over they rise and fall together; which means that where the people dwell who have reached the highest plane of excellence, there also are to be found the highest types of the musician and critic; and that in the degree in which the three factors, which united make up the sum of musical activity, labor harmoniously, conscientiously, and unselfishly, each striving to fulfil its mission, they advance music and further themselves, each bearing off an equal share of the good derived from the common effort. I have set the factors down in the order which they ordinarily occupy in popular discussion and which symbolizes their proper attitude toward each other and the highest potency of their collaboration. In this collaboration, as in so many others, it is conflict that brings life. Only by a surrender of their functions, one to the other, could the three apparently dissonant yet essentially harmonious factors be brought into a state of complacency; but such complacency would mean stagnation. If the published judgment on compositions and performances could always be that of the exploiting musicians, that class, at least, would read the newspapers with fewer heart-burnings; if the critics had a common mind and it were followed in concert-room and opera-house, they, as well as the musicians, would have need of fewer words of displacency and more of approbation; if, finally, it were to be brought to pass that for the public nothing but amiable diversion should flow simultaneously from platform, stage, and press, then for the public would the millennium be come. A religious philosopher can transmute Adam's fall into a blessing, and we can recognize the wisdom of that dispensation which put enmity between the seed of Jubal, who was the "father of all such as handle the harp and pipe," and the seed of Saul, who, I take it, is the first critic of record (and a vigorous one, too, for he accentuated his unfavorable opinion of a harper's harping with a javelin thrust).

[Sidenote: The critic an Ishmaelite.]

[Sidenote: The critic not to be pitied.]

[Sidenote: How he might extricate himself.]

[Sidenote: The public like to be flattered.]

We are bound to recognize that between the three factors there is, ever was, and ever shall be in sula sulorum an irrepressible conflict, and that in the nature of things the middle factor is the Ishmaelite whose hand is raised against everybody and against whom everybody's hand is raised. The complacency of the musician and the indifference, not to say ignorance, of the public ordinarily combine to make them allies, and the critic is, therefore, placed between two millstones, where he is vigorously rasped on both sides, and whence, being angular and hard of outer shell, he frequently requites the treatment received with complete and energetic reciprocity. Is he therefore to be pitied? Not a bit; for in this position he is performing one of the most significant and useful of his functions, and disclosing one of his most precious virtues. While musician and public must perforce remain in the positions in which they have been placed with relation to each other it must be apparent at half a glance that it would be the simplest matter in the world for the critic to extricate himself from his predicament. He would only need to take his cue from the public, measuring his commendation by the intensity of their applause, his dispraise by their signs of displeasure, and all would be well with him. We all know this to be true, that people like to read that which flatters them by echoing their own thoughts. The more delightfully it is put by the writer the more the reader is pleased, for has he not had the same idea? Are they not his? Is not their appearance in a public print proof of the shrewdness and soundness of his judgment? Ruskin knows this foible in human nature and condemns it. You may read in "Sesame and Lilies:"

"Very ready we are to say of a book, 'How good this is--that's exactly what I think!' But the right feeling is, 'How strange that is! I never thought of that before, and yet I see it is true; or if I do not now, I hope I shall, some day.' But whether thus submissively or not, at least be sure that you go at the author to get at his meaning, not to find yours. Judge it afterward if you think yourself qualified to do so, but ascertain it first."

[Sidenote: The critic generally outspoken.]

As a rule, however, the critic is not guilty of the wrong of speaking out the thought of others, but publishes what there is of his own mind, and this I laud in him as a virtue, which is praiseworthy in the degree that it springs from loftiness of aim, depth of knowledge, and sincerity and unselfishness of purpose.

[Sidenote: Musician and Public.]

[Sidenote: The office of ignorance.]

[Sidenote: _Popularity of Wagner's music not a sign of intelligent appreciation._]

Let us look a little into the views which our factors do and those which they ought to entertain of each other. The utterances of musicians have long ago made it plain that as between the critic and the public the greater measure of their respect and deference is given to the public. The critic is bound to recognize this as entirely natural; his right of protest does not accrue until he can show that the deference is ignoble and injurious to good art. It is to the public that the musician appeals for the substantial signs of what is called success. This appeal to the jury instead of the judge is as characteristic of the conscientious composer who is sincerely convinced that he was sent into the world to widen the boundaries of art, as it is of the mere time-server who aims only at tickling the popular ear. The reason is obvious to a little close thinking: Ignorance is at once a safeguard against and a promoter of conservatism. This sounds like a paradox, but the rapid growth of Wagner's music in the admiration of the people of the United States might correctly be cited as a proof that the statement is true. Music like the concert fragments from Wagner's lyric dramas is accepted with promptitude and delight, because its elements are those which appeal most directly and forcibly to our sense-perception and those primitive tastes which are the most readily gratified by strong outlines and vivid colors. Their vigorous rhythms, wealth of color, and sonority would make these fragments far more impressive to a savage than the suave beauty of a symphony by Haydn; yet do we not all know that while whole-hearted, intelligent enjoyment of a Haydn symphony is conditioned upon a considerable degree of culture, an equally whole-hearted, intelligent appreciation of Wagner's music presupposes a much wider range of sympathy, a much more extended view of the capabilities of musical expression, a much keener discernment, and a much profounder susceptibility to the effects of harmonic progressions? And is the conclusion not inevitable, therefore, that on the whole the ready acceptance of Wagner's music by a people is evidence that they are not sufficiently cultured to feel the force of that conservatism which made the triumph of Wagner consequent on many years of agitation in musical Germany?

[Sidenote: "Ahead of one's time."]

In one case the appeal is elemental; in the other spiritual. He who wishes to be in advance of his time does wisely in going to the people instead of the critics, just as the old fogy does whose music belongs to the time when sensuous charm summed up its essence. There is a good deal of ambiguity about the stereotyped phrase "ahead of one's time." Rightly apprehended, great geniuses do live for the future rather than the present, but where the public have the vastness of appetite and scantness of taste peculiar to the ostrich, there it is impossible for a composer to be ahead of his time. It is only where the public are advanced to the stage of intelligent discrimination that a Ninth Symphony and a Nibelung Tetralogy are accepted slowly.

[Sidenote: The charlatan.]

[Sidenote: Influencing the critics.]

Why the charlatan should profess to despise the critic and to pay homage only to the public scarcely needs an explanation. It is the critic who stands between him and the public he would victimize. Much of the disaffection between the concert-giver and the concert-reviewer arises from the unwillingness of the latter to enlist in a conspiracy to deceive and defraud the public. There is no need of mincing phrases here. The critics of the newspaper press are besieged daily with requests for notices of a complimentary character touching persons who have no honest standing in art. They are fawned on, truckled to, cajoled, subjected to the most seductive influences, sometimes bribed with woman's smiles or manager's money--and why? To win their influence in favor of good art, think you? No; to feed vanity and greed. When a critic is found of sufficient self-respect and character to resist all appeals and to be proof against all temptations, who is quicker than the musician to cite against his opinion the applause of the public over whose gullibility and ignorance, perchance, he made merry with the critic while trying to purchase his independence and honor?

[Sidenote: The public an elemental force.]

[Sidenote: Critic and public.]

[Sidenote: Schumann and popular approval.]

It is only when musicians divide the question touching the rights and merits of public and critic that they seem able to put a correct estimate upon the value of popular approval. At the last the best of them are willing, with Ferdinand Hiller, to look upon the public as an elemental power like the weather, which must be taken as it chances to come. With modern society resting upon the newspaper they might be willing to view the critic in the same light; but this they will not do so long as they adhere to the notion that criticism belongs of right to the professional musician, and will eventually be handed over to him. As for the critic, he may recognize the naturalness and reasonableness of a final resort for judgment to the factor for whose sake art is (i.e., the public), but he is not bound to admit its unfailing righteousness. Upon him, so he be worthy of his office, weighs the duty of first determining whether the appeal is taken from a lofty purpose or a low one, and whether or not the favored tribunal is worthy to try the case. Those who show a willingness to accept low ideals cannot exact high ones. The influence of their applause is a thousand-fold more injurious to art than the strictures of the most acrid critic. A musician of Schumann's mental and moral stature could recognize this and make it the basis of some of his most forcible aphorisms:

"'It pleased,' or 'It did not please,' say the people; as if there were no higher purpose than to please the people."

"The most difficult thing in the world to endure is the applause of fools!"

[Sidenote: Depreciation of the critic.]

[Sidenote: Value of public opinion.]

The belief professed by many musicians--professed, not really held--that the public can do no wrong, unquestionably grows out of a depreciation of the critic rather than an appreciation of the critical acumen of the masses. This depreciation is due more to the concrete work of the critic (which is only too often deserving of condemnation) than to a denial of the good offices of criticism. This much should be said for the musician, who is more liable to be misunderstood and more powerless against misrepresentation than any other artist. A line should be drawn between mere expression of opinion and criticism. It has been recognized for ages--you may find it plainly set forth in

Quintilian and Cicero--that in the long run the public are neither bad judges nor good critics. The distinction suggests a thought about the difference in value between a popular and a critical judgment. The former is, in the nature of things, ill considered and fleeting. It is the product of a momentary gratification or disappointment. In a much greater degree than a judgment based on principle and precedent, such as a critic's ought to be, it is a judgment swayed by that variable thing called fashion--"Qual pi' al vento."

[Sidenote: Duties of the critic.]

[Sidenote: The musician's duty toward the critic.]

But if this be so we ought plainly to understand the duties and obligations of the critic; perhaps it is because there is much misapprehension on this point that critics' writings have fallen under their own condemnation. I conceive that the first, if not the sole, office of the critic should be to guide public judgment. It is not for him to instruct the musician in his art. If this were always borne in mind by writers for the press it might help to soften the asperity felt by the musician toward the critic; and possibly the musician might then be persuaded to perform his first office toward the critic, which is to hold up his hands while he labors to steady and dignify public opinion. No true artist would give up years of honorable esteem to be the object for a moment of feverish idolatry. The public are fickle. "The garlands they twine," says Schumann, "they always pull to pieces again to offer them in another form to the next comer who chances to know how to amuse them better." Are such garlands worth the sacrifice of artistic honor? If it were possible for the critic to withhold them and offer instead a modest sprig of enduring bay, would not the musician be his debtor?

[Sidenote: The critic should steady public judgment.]

[Sidenote: Taste and judgment must be achieved.]

Another thought. Conceding that the people are the elemental power that Hiller says they are, who shall save them from the changeableness and instability which they show with relation to music and her votaries? Who shall bid the restless waves be still? We, in America, are a new people, a vast hotch-potch of varied and contradictory elements. We are engaged in conquering a continent; employed in a mad scramble for material things; we give feverish hours to win the comfort for our bodies that we take only seconds to enjoy; the moments which we steal from our labors we give grudgingly to relaxation, and that this relaxation may come quickly we ask that the agents which produce it shall appeal violently to the faculties which are most easily reached. Under these circumstances whence are to come the intellectual poise, the refined taste, the quick and sure power of analysis which must precede a correct estimate of the value of a composition or its performance?

"A taste or judgment," said Shaftesbury, "does not come ready formed with us into this world. Whatever principles or materials of this kind we may possibly bring with us, a legitimate and just taste can neither be begotten, made, conceived, or produced without the antecedent labor and pains of criticism."

[Sidenote: Comparative qualifications of critic and public.]

Grant that this antecedent criticism is the province of the critic and that he approaches even remotely a fulfilment of his mission in this regard, and who shall venture to question the value and the need of criticism to the promotion of public opinion? In this work the critic has a great advantage over the musician. The musician appeals to the public with volatile and elusive sounds. When he gets past the tympanum of the ear he works upon the emotions and the fancy. The public have no time to let him do more; for the rest they are willing to refer him to the critic, whose business it is continually to hear music for the purpose of forming opinions about it and expressing them. The critic has both the time and the obligation to analyze the reasons why and the extent to which the faculties are stirred into activity. Is it not plain, therefore, that the critic ought to be better able to distinguish the good from the bad, the true from the false, the sound from the meretricious, than the unindividualized multitude, who are already satisfied when they have felt the ticklings of pleasure?

[Sidenote: The critic's responsibilities.]

[Sidenote: Toward the musician.]

[Sidenote: Position and power of the newspaper.]

But when we place so great a mission as the education of public taste before the critic, we saddle him with a vast responsibility which is quite evenly divided between the musician and the public. The responsibility toward the musician is not that which we are accustomed to hear harped on by the aggrieved ones on the day after a concert. It is toward the musician only as a representative of art, and his just claims can have nothing of selfishness in them. The abnormal sensitiveness of the musician to criticism, though it may excite his commiseration and even honest pity, should never count with the critic in the performance of a plain duty. This sensitiveness is the product of a low state in music as well as criticism, and in the face of improvement in the two fields it will either disappear or fall under a killing condemnation. The power of the press will here work for good. The newspaper now fills the place in the musician's economy which a century ago was filled in Europe by the courts and nobility. Its support, indirect as well as direct, replaces the patronage which erstwhile came from these powerful ones. The evils which flow from the changed conditions are different in extent but not in kind from the old. Too frequently for the good of art that support is purchased by the same crookings of "the pregnant hinges of the knee" that were once the price of royal or noble condescension. If the tone of the press at times becomes arrogant, it is from the same causes that raised the voices and curled the lips of the petty dukes and princes, to flatter whose vanity great artists used to labor.

[Sidenote: _The musician should help to elevate the standard of criticism._]

[Sidenote: A critic must not necessarily be a musician.]

[Sidenote: Pedantry not wanted.]

The musician knows as well as anyone how impossible it is to escape the press, and it is, therefore, his plain duty to seek to raise the standard of its utterances by conceding the rights of the critic and encouraging honesty, fearlessness, impartiality, intelligence, and sympathy wherever he finds them. To this end he must cast away many antiquated and foolish prejudices. He must learn to confess with Wagner, the arch-enemy of criticism, that "blame is much more useful to the artist than praise," and that "the musician who goes to destruction because he is faulted, deserves destruction." He must stop the contention that only a musician is entitled to criticise a musician, and without abating one jot of his requirements as to knowledge, sympathy, liberality, broad-mindedness, candor, and incorruptibility on the part of the critic, he must quit the foolish claim that to pronounce upon the excellence of a ragout one must be able to cook it; if he will not go farther he must, at least, go with the elder D'Israeli to the extent of saying that "the talent of judgment may exist separately from the power of execution." One need not be a composer, but one must be able to feel with a composer before he can discuss his productions as they ought to be discussed. Not all the writers for the press are able to do this; many depend upon effrontery and a copious use of technical phrases to carry them through. The musician, alas! encourages this method whenever he gets a chance; nine times out of ten, when an opportunity to review a composition falls to him, he approaches it on its technical side. Yet music is of all the arts in the world the last that a mere pedant should discuss.

But if not a mere pedant, then neither a mere sentimentalist.

[Sidenote: Intelligence versus emotionalism.]

"If I had to choose between the merits of two classes of hearers, one of whom had an intelligent appreciation of music without feeling emotion; the other an emotional feeling without an intelligent analysis, I should unhesitatingly decide in favor of the intelligent non-emotionalist. And for these reasons: The verdict of the intelligent non-emotionalist would be valuable as far as it goes, but that of the untrained emotionalist is not of the smallest value; his blame and his praise are equally unfounded and empty."

[Sidenote: Personal equation.]

[Sidenote: Exact criticism.]

So writes Dr. Stainer, and it is his emotionalist against whom I uttered a warning in the introductory chapter of this book, when I called him a rhapsodist and described his motive to be primarily a desire to present himself as a person of unusually exquisite sensibilities. Frequently the rhapsodic style is adopted to conceal a want of knowledge, and, I fancy, sometimes also because ill-equipped critics have persuaded themselves that criticism being worthless, what the public need to read is a fantastic account of how music affects them. Now, it is true that what is chiefly valuable in criticism is what a man qualified to think and feel tells us he did think and feel under the inspiration of a performance; but when carried too far, or restricted too much, this conception of a critic's province lifts personal equation into dangerous prominence in the critical activity, and depreciates the elements of criticism, which are not matters of opinion or taste at all, but questions of fact, as exactly demonstrable as a problem in mathematics. In musical performance these elements belong to the technics of the art. Granted that the critic has a correct ear, a thing which he must have if he aspire to be a critic at all, and the possession of which is as easily proved as that of a dollar-bill in his pocket, the questions of justness of intonation in a singer or instrumentalist, balance of tone in an orchestra, correctness of phrasing, and many other things, are mere determinations of fact; the faculties which recognize their existence or discover their absence might exist in a person who is not "moved by concord of sweet sounds" at all, and whose taste is of the lowest type. It was the acoustician Euler, I believe, who said that he could construct a sonata according to the laws of mathematics--figure one out, that is.

[Sidenote: The Rhapsodists.]

[Sidenote: An English exemplar.]

Because music is in its nature such a mystery, because so little of its philosophy, so little of its science is popularly known, there has grown up the tribe of rhapsodical writers whose influence is most pernicious. I have a case in mind at which I have already hinted in this book--that of a certain English gentleman who has gained considerable eminence because of the loveliness of the subject on which he writes and his deftness in putting words together. On many points he is qualified to speak, and on these he generally speaks entertainingly. He frequently blunders in details, but it is only when he writes in the manner exemplified in the following excerpt from his book called "My Musical Memories," that he does mischief. The reverend gentleman, talking about violins, has reached one that once belonged to Ernst. This, he says, he sees occasionally, but he never hears it more except

[Sidenote: Ernst's violin.]

"In the night ... under the stars, when the moon is low and I see the dark ridges of the clover hills, and rabbits and hares, black against the paler sky, pausing to feed or crouching to listen to the voices of the night....

"By the sea, when the cold mists rise, and hollow murmurs, like the low wail of lost spirits, rush along the beach....

"In some still valley in the South, in midsummer. The slate-colored moth on the rock flashes suddenly into crimson and takes wing; the bright lizard darts timorously, and the singing of the grasshopper--"

[Sidenote: Mischievous writing.]

[Sidenote: Musical sensibility and sanity.]

Well, the reader, if he has a liking for such things, may himself go on for quantity. This is intended, I fancy, for poetical hyperbole, but as a matter of fact it is something else, and worse. Mr. Haweis does not hear Ernst's violin under any such improbable conditions; if he thinks he does he is a proper subject for medical inquiry. Neither does his effort at fine writing help us to appreciate the tone of the instrument. He did not intend that it should, but he probably did intend to make the reader marvel at the exquisite sensibility of his soul to music. This is mischievous, for it tends to make the injudicious think that they are lacking in musical appreciation, unless they, too, can see visions and hear voices and dream fantastic dreams when music is sounding. When such writing is popular it is difficult to make men and women believe that they may be just as susceptible to the influence of music as the child Mozart was to the sound of a trumpet, yet listen to it without once feeling the need of taking leave of their senses or wandering away from sanity. Moreover, when Mr. Haweis says that he sees but does not hear Ernst's violin more, he speaks most undeserved dispraise of one of the best violin players alive, for Ernst's violin now belongs to and is played by Lady Hall?-she that was Madame Norman-Neruda.

[Sidenote: A place for rhapsody.]

[Sidenote: Intelligent rhapsody.]

Is there, then, no place for rhapsodic writing in musical criticism? Yes, decidedly. It may, indeed, at times be the best, because the truest, writing. One would convey but a sorry idea of a composition were he to confine himself to a technical description of it--the number of its measures, its intervals, modulations, speed, and rhythm. Such a description would only be comprehensible to the trained musician, and to him would picture the body merely, not the soul. One might as well hope to tell of the beauty of a statue by reciting its dimensions. But knowledge as well as sympathy must speak out of the words, so that they may realize Schumann's lovely conception when he said that the best criticism is that which leaves after it an impression on the reader like that which the music made on the hearer. Read Dr. John Brown's account of one of Hall?s recitals, reprinted from "The Scotsman," in the collection of essays entitled "Spare Hours," if you would see how aptly a sweetly sane mind and a warm heart can rhapsodize without the help of technical knowledge:

[Sidenote: Dr. Brown and Beethoven.]

"Beethoven (Dr. Brown is speaking of the Sonata in D, op. 10, No. 3) begins with a trouble, a wandering and groping in the dark, a strange emergence of order out of chaos, a wild, rich confusion and misrule. Wilful and passionate, often harsh, and, as it were, thick with gloom; then comes, as if 'it stole upon the air,' the burden of the theme, the still, sad music--Largo e mesto--so human, so sorrowful, and yet the sorrow overcome, not by gladness but by something better, like the sea, after a dark night of tempest, falling asleep in the young light of morning, and 'whispering how meek and gentle it can be.' This likeness to the sea, its immensity, its uncertainty, its wild, strong glory and play, its peace, its solitude, its unsearchableness, its prevailing sadness, comes more into our minds with this great and deep master's works than any other."

That is Beethoven.

[Sidenote: Apollo and the critic--a fable.]

[Sidenote: The critic's duty to admire.]

[Sidenote: A mediator between musician and public.]

[Sidenote: Essential virtues.]

Once upon a time--it is an ancient fable--a critic picked out all the faults of a great poet and presented them to Apollo. The god received the gift graciously and set a bag of wheat before the critic with the command that he separate the chaff from the kernels. The critic did the work with alacrity, and turning to Apollo for his reward, received the chaff. Nothing could show us more appositely than this what criticism should not be. A critic's duty is to separate excellence from defect, as Dr. Crotch says; to admire as well as to find fault. In the proportion that defects are apparent he should increase his efforts to discover beauties. Much flows out of this conception of his duty. Holding it the critic will bring besides all needful knowledge a fulness of love into his work. "Where sympathy is lacking, correct judgment is also lacking," said Mendelssohn. The critic should be the mediator between the musician and the public. For all new works he should do what the symphonists of the Liszt school attempt to do by means of programmes; he should excite curiosity, arouse interest, and pave the way to popular comprehension. But for the old he should not fail to encourage reverence and admiration. To do both these things he must know his duty to the past, the present, and the future, and adjust each duty to the other. Such adjustment is only possible if he knows the music of the past and present, and is quick to perceive the bent and outcome of novel strivings. He should be catholic in taste, outspoken in judgment, unalterable in allegiance to his ideals, unswervable in integrity.

###

Printed in Great Britain
by Amazon